THE BROKEN MIRROR

Refracted Visions of Ourselves

JAMES HOLLIS, PH.D.

CHIRON PUBLICATIONS • ASHEVILLE, NORTH CAROLINA

www.ChironPublications.com

Interior and cover design by Danijela Mijailovic
Printed primarily in the United States of America.

ISBN978-1-68503-009-4 paperback
ISBN978-1-68503-010-0 hardcover
ISBN978-1-68503-011-7 electronic
ISBN978-1-68503-012-4 limited edition paperback

Library of Congress Cataloging-in-Publication Data Pending

This book is dedicated to my love, Jill,
whose painting graces this volume,
as well as three other Chiron Books.

And our children, Taryn and Timothy,
Jonah and Seah.

My abiding thanks also goes to Chiron friends:
Jennifer Fitzgerald
Steve Buser
Len Cruz

And my thanks to my friends, Carl Caldwell,
Constance and Robert Martindale, LaRue Owen,
Constance Avery-Clark, Bryon MacWilliams, and
Gail Hartman, who had a hand in this book.

Books by James Hollis

- *Harold Pinter: The Poetics of Silence*
- *The Middle Passage: From Misery to Meaning at Midlife*
- *Under Saturn's Shadow: The Wounding and Healing of Men*
- *Tracking the Gods: The Place of Myth in Modern Life*
- *Swamplands of the Soul: New Life from Dismal Places*
- *The Eden Project: In Search of the Magical Other*
- *The Archetypal Imagination Creating a Life: Finding Your Individual Path*
- *On This Journey We Call Our Life Mythologems: Incarnations of the Invisible World*
- *Finding Meaning in the Second Half of Life*
- *Why Good People Do Bad Things: Exploring Our Darker Selves*
- *What Matters Most - Living a More Considered Life*
- *Hauntings: Dispelling the Ghosts That Run Our Lives*
- *Living the Examined Life: Wisdom for the Second Half of the Journey*
- *Living Between Worlds: Finding Personal Resilience in Changing Times*
- *Prisms: Reflections on This Journey We Call Life*
- *The Best of James Hollis: Wisdom for the Inner Journey,* compiled by Logan Jones
- *The Broken Mirror: Refracted Visions of Ourselves*

Table of Contents

Preface   1

Chapter One: *Fear, Skepticism, Lassitude:*
    The Recovery of an Inner Life   5

Chapter Two: *The Zen Paradox: What You Have*
    Become is Now Your Chief Problem   25

Chapter Three: *Necessary Fictions: Therapy as*
    the Critique of "Stories"   45

Chapter Four: *Down and Out in Zürich: For Those Who*
    Think Becoming a Jungian Analyst is a Cool Thing   65

Chapter Five: *Shipwreck: The Importance of Failure*
    in Our Lives   77

Chapter Six: *Doing Difficult Therapy*   93

Chapter Seven: *Living in Haunted Houses: The Latest*
    News from the Madding Crowd Within   139

Chapter Eight: *The Gift, and the Limitations, of Therapy*   147

Chapter Nine: *Invisible Means of Support:*
    The Theogonies of Stephen Dunn   157

Chapter Ten: *The Resources Within Each of Us*   167

Chapter Eleven: *Notes Toward a Personal Memoir*   181

Afterword: *On the Matter of Soul*   201

Bibliography   207

Preface

"Always behind what we imagine our best deeds stands the devil, patting us paternally on the shoulder and whispering, 'Well done!'"

C. G. Jung, *CW 10*, "A Psychological View of Conscience," para. 837.

This collection of essays has arisen out of simultaneously responding to specific assignments presented by teaching venues, observing what is going on in the lives of analysands, and noting what is going on in mine. For example, the first three essays came from agreeing to reflect on the theme of "The Many Faces of Truth" presented by the *Jung on the Hudson* program in the summer of 2021. Given that rich title, which instantly reminds us that truth is seldom objectively discernible, yet always subjectively experienced, three topics flowed before my mind's eye very quickly. And so, respectively, they offer a taxonomy of 1) our internal obstacles to knowing ourselves and our world: fear, skepticism, and lassitude, 2) our captivation by our necessary adaptations to the environment around us, and 3) our possession by our "stories" whereby we seek to make sense of our lives.

In different ways, these essays address the gulf between the world "out there," and the world in us which receives, processes, and re-construes it. All of us are children of David Hume in Edinburgh, Scotland and Immanuel Kant in

1

Königsberg, Prussia who by the beginning of the nineteenth century had convincingly demonstrated that we do not know things in themselves but rather our interior facsimiles of them.

You and I can look at the same orange, experience quite different realities, and swim in a field of "orangeness" quite unique to each of us. Having ended the essential work of *metaphysics*, the identification of "reality," philosophers were still left with *epistemology*—how do we know, what are the limits of knowing—and *axiology*, what do we do with what we believe we know. This philosophical pivot also begat the discipline of phenomenology which explores the conditions of sensation, perception, and image formation. That, and the collapse of tribal and institutional mythologies all around led, as Jung pointed out, to the necessary "invention" of depth psychology by the end of that same century. He, Freud, Adler, and others at the turn of the next century introduced us to the study of the unconscious, and speculated on means by which we might begin to dialogue with, and interrogate, what by definition was unknown to us. Following these scattered breadcrumbs that lead through psyche's forest is the continuing project of both the modern and post-modern worlds.

Through all this rich ruin of a long tradition of "certainty," the human ego is repeatedly obliged to relinquish its presumptive throne and deal with the fact that our restive peasants down below are in revolt, and no one really knows what lies around the next turn of history. I have always been pleasantly haunted by the melancholy poetry of the King James version of the Bible, especially the line in the First Letter of Paul to the Corinthians: 13:12. *"For now we see through a glass, darkly, but then face to face; now I know in part, but then shall I know even as I am known."* Whether we are "known" by God, as Paul believed, or by our own psyche as many contemporaries believe, there is something within each of us that knows more than we know, knows us better than we know ourselves, and seemingly is seeking to catalyze a conversation with consciousness, sending forth dreams, symptoms, and revelatory events to crash upon the ego's permeable membranes. For most of us on our planet in this time, the mirror is broken, and we get only refracted slivers of re-cognition from time to time. If that is all we get, we had better take them seriously then.

In my 82nd year, I know more than I have ever known, and I now know less than I knew as a child. I have given up on the idea of peace of mind. I think too much is turbulent, too much rapidly moving for that. Back in the 1970's I was sitting in a class at the *Jung-Institut* in Zürich, Switzerland. There I heard for the first time the paragraph which asked a question that only some original imagination like Jung would have thought of asking. Where, he queried, did the gods go when they left Olympus? If they are gods, they are eternal by definition—so where are Zeus, Hera, Aphrodite, Ares, Apollo, Artemis, and all that shining assembly today? He posited that the energy that once illumined and activated those names had long departed and gone elsewhere. Thus, we recognize that the "gods" are "energies," not anthropomorphic entities looking down on this tattered planet. He argued further that they left Mt. Olympus and entered the solar plexus of the modern, and there, neglected, disowned, they pathologize and become the diseases of our age and of our person.

At that moment, I knew what my thesis in Zürich would be: figuring out where those timeless energies went. About the same time, I was reading Rilke's *Sonnets to Orpheus* in German, and in one poem the speaker records the fleeting intimation that Apollo had just passed, leaving *nur ein spur* (only a trace). So, I thought of the metaphor "tracing" the gods, but it didn't seem vigorous, or rigorous enough; and so the title became *Tracking the Gods*, and later an expanded book of the same title. Tracking where the energy presently manifests in a person's life tells us where we need to bring consciousness, and accountability along with it.

As I wrote in *Living Between Worlds*, "the gods have departed and left us to our own devices, and it's not going so well. We work assiduously at denial, convinced of our purblind assertions of certainty, partaking of a thousand distracting, numbing, addictive, seductive treatment plans that leave us so palpably alone, so lonely, and so terribly full of longing."[1]

These essays, then, are all about tracking the movement of the spirit world through the forms of our material world. It is the project to which depth psychology has devoted itself, and a project which brings renewed energy, momentum, discovery, and larger horizons to each of us. I hope that these essays contribute in some way to your reflections on where those energies are tracking in your life.

James Hollis, Ph.D.
Washington, DC
2021

---

[1] Hollis, *Living Between Worlds*, p. 190.

CHAPTER ONE

Fear, Skepticism, Lassitude:
The Recovery of an Inner Life

Resistance is always in due proportion to the anxiety generated by some invitation or challenge. Inside of each of us is continuing civil conflict, and typically our protective instincts are easily intimidated by the magnitude of the tasks life brings us. Moreover, we are often flooded with skepticism regarding our inherent resources for the trial, and an internal aversion to the struggle. These engagements, these battles of outer and inner worlds, are only resolved when we are led to a change of attitude, a riskier but more considered intent, and a consistent, daily showing up to tilt the balance between regression and progression.

When therapists talk with each other, or do case supervision, they often puzzle over the paradox that their clients come to them seeking change in their lives, and resist that change with all their powers. We all know that resistance is found in direct proportion to the amount of fear generated. Jung noted that most of his patients arrived at their first hour having some sense of what issues, and what tasks, awaited them. Elsewhere he said therapists should always reflect upon the question: What accountability is this person's life helping him or her avoid? Then, too, many think that the therapist has some sort of magic to dispense, either as a result of their having solved similar dilemmas in their lives, or as imparted to them in some arcane set of steps, attitudes, practices during their period of professional training. A number of years ago, in a book titled *Creating a Life*, I asserted that few folks would come to therapy, and fewer still remain in treatment, if truth in advertising were really a part of the therapist's code of ethics.

Full professional disclosure would oblige the therapist to inform all new clients of the following realities:

First, you will have to deal with this core issue the rest of your life, and at best you will manage to win a few skirmishes in your long uncivil war with yourself. Decades from now you will be fighting on these familiar fronts, though the terrain may have shifted so much that you may have difficulty recognizing the same old, same old.

Second, you will be obliged to disassemble the many forces you have gathered to defend against your wound. At this late date it is your defenses, not your wound that cause the problem and arrest your journey. But removing those defenses will oblige you to feel all the discomfort of that wound again.

And third, you will not be spared pain, vouchsafed wisdom or granted exemption from future suffering.[2]

Having read those three paragraphs, a friend of mine in Houston said, "Well, that will end the self-help genre for good." In the lines that follow, I went on to agree that the nature of this work does belie the facile claims of so many on behalf of short-term therapy when studies of long-term therapy reveal much better outcomes. But what this work will give you, if not surcease from the long twilight struggle

---

[2] Hollis, *Creating a Life: Finding Your Individual Path*, pp. 18-9.

for independence from history, is a more interesting life. That may seem small reward for such sustained and intensive work, but a greater consciousness around the engines that run our lives, the places where our awareness and resolve can make a difference, and the summons to partnership with our own souls on behalf of the depth and dignity of self-direction is an incalculable gift.

In his 1912 book *Symbols of Transformation*, Jung describes the universal tension between the psyche's desire for progression or regression. When we awaken in the morning, a part of us wishes to remain in the nether word of sleep, protected from the conflicts inherent in life, and floating in a foggy cloud. Our ancestors, he notes, knew this temptation, this pattern quite well and as a result they originated those great "psychotherapeutic systems" we call the religions, myths, and rites of passage. In each, symbols carry the power to arouse, move, even guide libido, or psychic energy, in service to development, and without which, the species would remain infantile, perhaps even perish when faced with the rigorous demands of nature.

At the same time, the message we all learned from childhood was the existential gap between what we narcissistically desire and our powers of achieving it. In so many words, *"The world is big, and you are not; the world is powerful, and you are not. Now, just deal with that fact for a few decades."* The overt legacy of that message is that we lack the capacity to take the world on, must hide out, and hope for rescue from some benevolent other. Poet Anne Sexton recalls this intimidation so well, and reports her thoughts at the time, providing us with a window into our forgotten childhood terrors.

It is dark,
where are the big people,
when will I get there,
taking giant steps
all day,
each day
and thinking
nothing of it?[3]

This twin combination, fear and lethargy (or lassitude) is present to us any moment, often making choices for us, and removing us from the struggle for life, and for enacting our desires into the world. Many years ago in *The Middle Passage*, I personified these force-fields as twin gremlins who sit at the foot of our bed each morning. One intimidates, one seduces us into slumber. They are the enemies of life, and we carry them within us everywhere we go; and if we stand up to their challenge today, they will be there again tomorrow waiting for us to open our eyes. We may fear the hosts of evil and intimidation around us, but our biggest obstacle will always remain within. And there they will be, at the foot of the bed, smirking, and waiting for us to awaken from troubled sleep and take them on again.

Nonetheless, there is within each of us, a constellation of energy Jung called "the archetype of the hero," the carrier of desire into the world despite the intimidations of the world. The spirit of evil, he notes, is the negation of the life force by fear, or its seduction by lethargy. And only by risking these compelling powers can we live the meaningful life, that is to say, not get our way, but serve the life that wishes expression through us.

---

[3] https://allpoetry.com/The-Fury-Of-Overshoes

For example, those who study the creative process reverse the way in which most people see creativity.[4] Most folks think that the artist "has something to say." Those who do embody that premise more often turn out to be preachers, politicians, and soap salesmen of some kind, for their rhetorical agendas prevail over a visitation by the muse or the *Daimon*. A former colleague of mine longed for a month in a remote cabin in Maine to finish her novel. When she finally wangled a way to find that cabin, she emerged after thirty days with a log detailing all the excuses that she found—good reasons, bad reasons, distractions—that prevented her from achieving anything worth keeping. Her written description of that process was both humorous and painful. On the other hand, artists themselves emphasize the labor it takes, the willingness to sacrifice creature comforts, the need for discipline which calls one to stand before the soul's smithy and its challenge one more time, one more day. Sports writer Red Smith said writing was easy—all one has to do is sit before the keyboard and open a vein. Historian Hilary Mantel expresses her irritation at those who assume writing is easy for her. Instead she describes how constant vigilance is required to respond to any prompting which rises out of her project, and a willingness to submit to it. The late painter Chuck Close who suffered a catastrophic illness, and completely revised his subjects and techniques said, "Inspiration is for amateurs. The rest of us just show up and get to work." My own experience of writing eighteen books and two dissertations is often analogous to being gripped by something that lays hold of me, and to which I am compelled to submit. It is never easy;

---

[4] For example, see Lorne Buchman's fine study of creativity *Make to Know* which queries the creative process and creators to find that they did not know what their work was "saying," but only that something needed saying, and they became its channel into the world.

it is never fun, though there is a marvelous moment when the right word falls into place. Thomas Mann said that writing was especially difficult for those who write. For those who say they want to write, compose, paint, I always think, "Welcome to the sweat shop—but it is real sweat that will be asked of you. Are you up for that?"

I was once asked if I thought the relationship of the ego to the unconscious was roughly fifty/fifty. I replied that the ego is a tiny, frangible wafer tossed about on a tenebrous sea. As every mariner knows, our boat is so small and the sea is so large. I have in front of me a nineteenth century Swiss postcard of the Rhein Falls and the Alps in the distance. Jung was born very near here. From this old photo one can see an immense panorama—one sees with the eye of God, one might say. I remember standing at the edge of those same falls and feeling dwarfed by the roaring tumult that filled and fused the senses. Any picture we have of things is but a frame, and the mysterious Other is always larger than the frame we can imagine. Holding to that ego frame, and yet not shutting off the magnitude of the Other, is a tricky balance, whether one is an artist, or a person trying to make sense of life.

If the central message to all of us that the world out there is big, and we are not, so too the immensity of the world within dwarfs and intimidates this fragile assemblage we call consciousness. In his poem "Desert Places," Robert Frost put it this way,

> They cannot scare me with their empty spaces
> Between stars - on stars where no human race is.
> I have it in me so much nearer home
> To scare myself with my own desert places.[5]

---

[5] https://www.poemhunter.com/poem/desert-places/

We have within us vast oceans of space, swirling energies, tumult-driven engines of desire, fearsome abysses, and vaults of soaring aspiration. Every time I hear another well-coifed evangelist proclaiming his special access to the messages of Divinity, I wonder what cluster of insecurity, or seductive inflation, has his ego in its grip. Any ego not dwarfed by the magnitude within is simply non-reflective, or unconscious altogether. It is an abiding respect for this disproportionate relationship between the ego and the unconscious that no doubt led Jung, when asked for the thousandth time, his definition of *God*, sometimes called *The Wholly Other*, to reply: "To this day *God* is the name by which I designate all things which cross my willful path violently and recklessly, all things which upset my subjective views, plans and intentions and change the course of my life for better or worse."[6] It's a strange definition, but manifests a deeply humble respect for the mystery, and an acknowledgement that our theologies, and psychologies, are limited by the constrictions of our rational and imaginative capacities. Accordingly, anything we say of such ungraspables reveals more about us than the mystery. His respect for the mystery did not, however, prevent him from undertaking explorations into the "unknowable," and to develop methods for tracking the passing of the invisible as it moves through the cerements of the visible, fleeting material forms of our brief lives.

It is easy enough to see how quickly our ego is overwhelmed and intimidated by the magnitude of the project the enlargement of consciousness requires. Moreover, we are often flooded with skepticism regarding our inherent resources for the trial, as well as an internal aversion

---

[6] https://thesethingsinside.wordpress.com/2013/01/07/carl-jung-says-god-is-reality-itself/

to the struggle. I can recall lying on the grass when I was a child, and staring into the curving vault of the sky above me. (Much later, I was reminded of that timeless moment when I first read Shelley's description of the vaulted "dome of many colored glass" above him.) I thought for a moment, what if this world in which I am is but a drop of fluid, a cell in the mind of a great dreamer? And this Great Dreamer is dreaming the dream in which I believe my life exists. And what if, it quickly followed, that dreamer woke up, or dreamt another world—what would happen to me? As I best recall, I was not frightened by that vertiginous prospect, but I did sense how tiny I was and how dependent upon the vast powers beyond me.

In the long years which have followed, I have studied many maps of the universe, and still that old conundrum persists. Back in the seventeenth century, the mathematician and mystic Blaise Pascal must have had a similar image come to him when he described the human psyche as a reed easily snapped by the rigors of natural life, and yet a thinking reed that could nonetheless conjure with the universe that could so casually destroy him. Later, the Romantic poet Samuel Taylor Coleridge asked this question: "What if in your sleep you dreamed, and what if in your dream you went to heaven and there plucked a strange and beautiful flower, and what if when you awoke you had the flower in your hand?"[7] Hmm....heart mysteries there for all of us.

No wonder so many folks wait upon some charismatic prophet, or itinerant guru, to bring them a fleshed-out summary of the Big Picture. It's much easier to absorb a picture ready-made than to explore those labyrinthine passages of the soul to find our own. No wonder no era has

---

[7] https://quoteinvestigator.com/2017/05/29/flower/

ever been without its charlatans, its inflated true-believers, and its Yankee Doodle flim-flamers because they spare us so much work. No wonder the Grand Inquisitor in Dostoevsky's parable *The Brothers Karamazov*, admonished the returned Jesus that his way of the cross will never capture the souls of humanity as successfully as those who own and manipulate miracle, mystery, and authority. Some days it's enough to get out of bed; why should one have to wrestle with the existential riddles that stir our dreams and disrupt our daily schedules? Struggling with all this stuff is just hard work, and there must be an easier way. There is an old saying that the Devil does his best work by whispering in our ears what we really want to hear. No wonder he is so successful in telling us in so many ways how there *is* an easy path, with a guaranteed payoff.

We also grow skeptical of our chances of wrestling with the magnitude of this journey because we have so many setbacks. Even those who work earnestly are accustomed to finding themselves in the same-old rut. How many analysands have expressed grave chagrin, abiding reservations about the idea of psychological progress? Jung himself noted this frequent disappointment to the ego. "I have treated many patients who were conscious of the cause of their complexes down to the last detail, without having been helped in any way by this insight."[8]

Nothing we have ever experienced is wholly lost. It is ingrained somewhere in our neurology and stored in the vaults of the unconscious even if it is not available to memory. These layers of charged history within us may help us cope with life's ever-changing demands, or they may impose

---

[8] Jung, *CW 8*, para. 714.

upon the new setting the data, story, and instructional script of the old, thus prejudicing the new, and creating our behavioral patterns. Our biographies are thus the Paleolithic layers of our complexes which from time to time we can explore as we once explored the pre-Neanderthal caves in the Dordogne. While we have a chronological age to denote our time on the surface of this planet, some of those layers, as Jung discovered, are timeless and link us to a kinship with all humans who have walked this earth. While we could never exhaust this vast thesaurus any more than we could empty the ocean with a bucket in hand, our engagements, conversations, and queries with the unconscious are typically the richest conversations we will ever have.

Recently I was asked whether the unconscious itself has a consciousness. (Who, or what, for example, is talking to us through our dreams?) It is an impossible question to answer, though it is abundantly clear that there is an intentionality to the unconscious. Seemingly, it seeks first our growth and development, whether we so wish them or not. This "development" moves us from the original zygote through the seasons of our lives and includes our progressive desiccation and demise. While the ego may have an attitude about this process, its opinions are irrelevant to the movement of our naturally unfolding plan. Secondly, the unconscious seems to seek the healing of whatever traumata may befall us. Medicine does not mend the broken bone or heal the effect of life's hammer-blows, but it can further the conditions in which that mystery of healing can occur. Thus the physician is a priest in service to the Great Mother archetype, which is the engine of birth, death, rebirth that courses through us at all times. Modernism may arrogate to itself the powers of the gods, but in the end, the work of the gods will always humble, surprise, and invite us to the next layer of mystery.

If the unconscious has an "intentionality," as I have conservatively described it, it nonetheless invites dialogue and dialectic with the conscious sphere. This very invitation is often intimidating. That we have shadows is ample proof of our desire to bury the evidence, gloss over the implications, and often speaks to us like a British Bobby on patrol at the scene of the crime: "Move along, folks. Nothing to see here." When Oedipus vows to find the criminal whose acts have somehow triggered the malaise that has befallen Thebes, even if the culprit's tracks lead back to the palace, his complicit mother quickly offers distraction, telling him that many have had such disturbing dreams and intimations, and they are to be dismissed as piffles, mere wills of the wisp. In other words, "Let us shut the investigation down." But Oedipus persists, and has the strength to face what may finally be unfaceable—the miscreant he seeks is himself. In one of his volumes, Jung writes that the dread and resistance to exploring our own depths is understandable for it may require of us a voyage to Hades.[9]

There has been a tendency to romanticize the un-conscious, to approach it as an aesthetic event, a parlor game, a pleasant stroll in the park. But we are animals, walking, talking, complex animals and what lies within us is primal nature with its amoral agenda. In each of us is the murderer, the cheat, the coward, the liar, the betrayer, a beast with blood on its fangs, even as a saint may also be found among that motley crew. As Roman playwright Terence noted over two millennia ago, "Nothing human is alien to me." If we disown, repress our natural state, and its cast of saints and ruffians, or project them on to others, we once again have fled a humbling invitation to self-awareness. Do

---

[9] Jung, *CW 12. Psychology and Alchemy*, para. 439.

we really want to know ourselves? Can we bear that? Poet Maxine Kumin dramatizes this ambivalent inquiry into what lies in our psychic basements in her poem "Woodchucks." What if those noisome stirrings down below, which we wish to dominate, dismiss, disown, require us to look at ourselves in a new and troubling way? What, O what then shall we do?

> Gassing the woodchucks didn't turn out right.
> The knockout bomb from the Feed and Grain Exchange
> was featured as merciful, quick at the bone
> and the case we had against them was airtight,
> both exits shoehorned shut with puddingstone,
> but they had a sub-sub-basement out of range.
> Next morning they turned up again, no worse
> for the cyanide than we for our cigarettes
> and state-store Scotch, all of us up to scratch.
>
> They brought down the marigolds as a matter of course
> and then took over the vegetable patch
> nipping the broccoli shoots, beheading the carrots.
> The food from our mouths, I said, righteously thrilling
> to the feel of the .22, the bullets' neat noses.
> I, a lapsed pacifist fallen from grace
> puffed with Darwinian pieties for killing,
> now drew a bead on the little woodchuck's face.
> He died down in the everbearing roses.
> Ten minutes later I dropped the mother. She
> flipflopped in the air and fell, her needle teeth
> still hooked in a leaf of early Swiss chard.
> Another baby next. O one-two-three
> the murderer inside me rose up hard,
> the hawkeye killer came on stage forthwith.
> There's one chuck left. Old wily fellow, he keeps

me cocked and ready day after day after day.
All night I hunt his humped-up form. I dream
I sight along the barrel in my sleep.
If only they'd all consented to die unseen
gassed underground the quiet Nazi way.[10]

If we are so often reluctant visitors to the mouth of the huge cave we all carry within, what makes us engage this inquiry with urgency? Why, for example, did Jung voyage to his Hades in *The Red Book*, dialogue and paint its lineaments, and finally return to his quotidian world of family, practice, academic discourse? Often the answer is *necessity*, driven by our dismay over our actions and their consequences. Often the irruption of autonomous pathology, a depression, and addiction, obliges this forensic inquiry. My early adult life was driven by intellectual curiosity and led me to complete a doctorate before I was 27, but down below, other incendiary guerillas bided their time, fomented discord in the canebrakes, performed acts of sabotage in the circuitry of my acquired life, and in my early thirties stormed the Capitol. That is what led me, reluctantly, to my first hour of analysis, and ultimately to Zürich, not as a planned change of career, but as a need to get to the bottom of these uncivil wars. As friend Daryl Sharp said, "All of us entered Zürich on our knees." He didn't mean as supplicant pilgrims might visit a religious shrine but as broken, hurting, sometimes desperate fugitives.

Remembering that the etymology of "psychopathology" means "the expression of the suffering of the soul," we then realize that what is transpiring is a crisis of stories, a conflict of myths, and polarized parties in contention for sovereignty

---

[10] https://poets.org/poem/woodchucks

over the soul. It wasn't just that I was curious to explore what was erupting from within, I had to attend this insurgency or die. Marie-Louise von Franz used to quote the medieval aphorism, "Suffering is the fastest horse to completion." I am not sure about the completion part, but suffering certainly gets our attention. For a while, after I was living in Zürich, I didn't really know why I was there, but I was following some breadcrumbs through a dark forest that ultimately led me to reticulated deaths and rebirths, occasional insights, and always to a confrontation with myself with all its unfinished business. Once begun seriously, that work never ends. Never begun, life is already finished, and only dull repetitions trail behind us.

Once we have outlived the story that brought us this far, and after our futile efforts to revive its compelling power, then we have that terrible "in-between," that no-man's land. It is the in-between of stories that is most difficult with our informing maps lost, in between gods, and in-between understandings of self and world. Even when our adaptations were shabby simulacrums of life, they offered a clarity, a certainty, and a set of familiar marching orders. Take them away and we are flooded with anxiety, or numbed by depression, or both. I recall two specific occasions where I went to analysis and sat there before the analyst, waited for something to say, stupefied before my own Gordian knots, found nothing, and respectfully withdrew until our next session. On one occasion, when I was in the final boarding process for a round of eight hour-long oral diploma exams by specialists in the topics being tested when my analyst said, "You know, you would be better off if you never read another book." And on another occasion, "Go to one of the ends of the fourteen tramlines in Zürich, get off and walk in the forests there. The Great Mother will heal you." There are hours in one's life, in most folk's life, which are truly desolate. Hanging on is what one has to do. Churchill said that when one find's oneself lost in a dark wood, keep walking. Jung said that at the bottom of every depression, and there is always a bottom there, one will find a task, the addressing of which will take one's life in a new direction. And so I, and so many others, have found directives arising from those most dismal soul-swamps.

Having overlearned the powerlessness of childhood, having turned away from so many challenges heretofore, we find it difficult to believe that we have that tensile strength necessary for death and rebirth. (This is what I call the "*Moi* Complex," as in *moi*? Me?). Intuitively, I knew that I was where I needed to be, and what I needed to do, even though no one else could understand. The loneliness of that place is where the soul is found. Something carries us through. Albert Camus found this for himself: "In the midst of winter, I found there was, within me, an invincible summer. And that makes me happy. For it says that no matter how hard the world pushes against me, within me, there's something stronger – something better, pushing right back."

When one discovers, really discovers in a felt way, that there is something there, some intentionality pushing back in a substantive way, then one's attitude begins to change. One is then invited to begin a relationship of trust. But that trust will not come to us without risk. I recall walking out of analysis at the end of my fourth year in Zürich having had one more dream speak the same message to me. If I had been there four years, I was clearly committed and doing the work, but there was also something, some doubt perhaps, kept in reserve, some voice whispering "this is all folly." But I could not refute what I had seen. A dream is not something we choose or direct. It is something that comes to us like a foreign visitor. It is a confrontation with that mysterious Other that abides within. At that moment, something shifted inside me, moving metaphorically from the conviction of the mind to a felt experience of the heart. And from that moment on I knew that I, too, had an invincible summer in me.

Jung noted that what we call "neurosis," a deep inner split between our instincts and our acclimated acculturations, is a suffering that has not yet found its meaning. In those dark hours I found, and so many have found, meaning that transcends whatever the losses, whatever the disappointments, whatever the discarded expectations.

Nietzsche had earlier contended that we can live with any suffering if we have a "why" that provides us a meaningful perspective on it. This existential rapprochement does not satisfy the wishes of the ego, of course, which is one reason why Jung's psychology will never really be popular. It does not offer a key to the promised land, or even a surcease of suffering. What psychology will ever be popular if it does not offer the former ego position a better deal, at least a trade off? Any psychology which asks us to die, in some profound fashion, will never tempt the mass market from its deceptive but seductive soporifics.

Accordingly, Jung noted, any real shift in a person's psychological frame will require of the ego a significant if not apocalyptic change of attitude. Our ego-state exhibits fundamentalist tendencies; terrified by ambiguity, it wishes for clarity, certainty, control. Such an agenda is understandable because it is always a treatment plan for the ego's nervousness, but it is also doomed to failure because larger life lies beyond such puny measures. (This is why so many raised in fundamentalist traditions suffer so much, and are so fervid in their avowals of belief. Their psyches have already moved beyond impoverished panaceas of palliative prophecy, and yet the ego remains timorous, and resistant, forgetting that their various founders once said, "Unless ye die, ye shall not live.")

Jung put it this way, "There is a widespread prejudice that analysis is something like a 'cure,' to which one submits for a time and then is discharged healed...Analytical treatment could be described as a readjustment of psychological attitude achieved with the help of the doctor." This adjustment does not mean that life is smooth thereafter. The complexity and autonomy of life are such that it remains forever beyond our control. Moreover, the phantasy of "cure" is a misnomer. Life is not a disease, and a neurosis is not a cancer to be excised. Any seeming resolution today will have to be revised tomorrow for the psyche is a flowing river, and yesterday's resolution is tomorrow's constriction. For this reason, Jung added, "There is no change that is unconditionally valid over a long period of time. Life always has to be tackled anew."

If we understand, at least provisionally, what we are doing, and why we are doing it, the ego can often tilt the balance in favor of enlargement rather than diminishment. A frequent question we may ask of ourselves at any critical juncture of choice is precisely that:*will this path, this choice enlarge me or will it diminish me?* Usually, we immediately know the answer to the question. If we don't, but persist asking, the answer will come to us. Here we see the role the ego may play in the presence of the large intimidating forces which contend within us. As a very mundane example: I am a card-carrying introvert and yet do a lot of public speaking. I began teaching at the college level at age 25, but to this day, I have what I call my "neurasthenic fit" before speaking. I ache all over; I have no energy, and I am convinced that I have nothing to say that is not already known by everyone. And yet, life calls, and what will we feel like if we have a calling and fail to show up? Is it not far worse to run from our fears and suffer the slow seep of inauthenticity into our lives? We all *do* have a calling, the summons to individuation, the assignment to carry into this world, in our short span on earth, whatever the gods intended for us. This is one place where consciousness can and does play a role and sometimes really can tip the balance. So, I say to myself, "Stop whining. This is just your neurosis, allied with voices from the past. This is the price of the ticket to life. No ticket, no life."

The soul always knows, and pathologizes in protest when we flag or fail. And who would ever have imagined that we might actually be led to consider psychopathology a friend of ours, for it is the tocsin, the warning bell that tells us we are violating the soul's imperative. Acknowledging and tracking these expressions of the psyche's dismay is how the ego can learn to live in a greater harmony with its other, disparate entities. Our psychopathology promotes an ecology of the soul, so to speak. And, now warned, now alerted, the ego has a summons to accountability, an accountability to the soul's agenda.

Every day is a summons to larger life. Every day a combat between the forces of *regression*—to fall back into the sleep of naiveté, dependency, unconsciousness—and *progression* to carry on the mystery of our human incarnation further into the unknown but fallow fields of the possible human.

Fear, skepticisms, and lassitude contend within all of us, and yet too the same energy surges that sent our ancestors across those tumultuous seas to the new world waiting for them, knowing they would never see home and loved ones again. Like Tennyson's Ulysses, we carry the same genetic code that drove that ancient salt-soaked, surf-wracked mariner, and carried his "gray spirit yearning in desire / to follow knowledge like a sinking star, beyond the utmost bound of human thought." His mission took him all the way home. Such missions, and such Ithakas, wait for all of us, daring us to show up as best we can, and some day find our way back home to ourselves.

CHAPTER TWO

The Zen Paradox: What You Have Become is Now Your Chief Problem

Creatures of infinite adaptation as we are, our historic accommodations with the world constitute a prejudicing of each new moment, and a potential sabotage of the developmental challenges of later life. It is humbling to realize that what worked for us historically, now limits us to the disempowered, constricted messages of history. Given that relinquishing our protections causes unacceptable anxiety, we are predisposed to repetition, rationalizations, and stuckness. Only when we recognize this reflexive claim upon us from our past, can we access the resolve to break through into the growth the soul is asking of us.

Robert Frost once wrote, "Forgive O Lord my little joke on thee, and I'll forgive Thy great big joke on me." One senses that Frost, popularly known as the sagacious old Vermont poet, has a beef with the Party of the First Part, but he also admits that he is unlikely to receive clarification, or figure out what the point of the joke was. Similarly, Samuel Beckett places his two characters, resembling Laurel and Hardy on a bad day, in *Waiting for Godot* on a sterile plain, and then spends two hours having them speculate on why they are there, what they should do about it, and who, if anyone, might be approaching to sort it all out for them. Most people assumed Beckett was referencing an age between Divine Dispensations, and that the two tramps wait for clarity and rescue from God, any God, but Beckett said "If I meant God, I would have said *God*." In the original French in which he wrote the play, Charlot was the familiar sobriquet for their beloved Charlie Chaplin, the "Little Tramp." So if that "god" were to appear, it might be more chaplinesque than the Omnipotent rumors would lead us to expect.

British playwright Harold Pinter wrote a play I saw off-Broadway about 1965 called *The Dumbwaiter*. In it, two bum-like hitmen wait in the basement for their assignment. As they wait, absurd orders for exquisite meals clatter down the dumbwaiter. Not wanting to reveal their nefarious mission, they send up what miserable meals they can cobble together from their packed lunches. As the demands upon them grow greater, more absurd, they finally cry upstairs that their resources are exhausted, they can offer up nothing more. (Notice the puns in the title: they are dumb/ignorant, unable to speak, and their only action is to wait till they are informed about the bigger picture.) Then comes the message that the person to be murdered is one of them, and his partner the designated assassin. It is not much of an allegoric stretch to see the two waiting on the lower level for clarity, reaching instead exhaustion of their resources, and being abandoned on a killing field as something of a reminder of the divine disconnect so many contemporaries experience from a nurturing, protective link to a larger order, a clarifying story, a transcendent Other. Remember also, Jung shaking his passionate fist at Yahweh in his *Answer to Job*. In all of these cases, the human is left without access to the big picture, without clarity of purpose, and is obliged to adapt to survive. Sometimes we humans have only our adaptations, without understanding why, in service to what, and how it may fit into a larger story, or even if there is a larger story.

There is an irony here. That we are still here, our branch of the many that started and faltered in the harsh conditions of this spinning planet, is owing precisely to our capacity to adapt. Adaptation is survival; failure to adapt is annihilation. Consider the work of my friend the nature writer Barbara Hurd. In her latest book *The Epilogues: Afterwards on the Planet*, a lament for the glories of the earth already slipping out of our reach, she cites a personal example. While swimming with those large, lumbering turtles in the Galapagos, reaching the size of small hippos, she learned that the mother instinctively leaves her protection in the roiling sea and clambers up on the beach where she is totally at the mercy of her predators. She deposits the eggs, retreats into the surf, and the eggs are there for eight weeks to mature. When deposited, their sex is undetermined. Below 80-some degrees Fahrenheit, the egg will produce a boy. Above that number, a girl will emerge. With global warming upon us, the recent ration of girls to boys is approximately ninety-nine to one percent. Barbara notes, no species can survive this gender discrepancy, and this wondrous creature will soon be a memory in our lamentable catalogue of human destruction. While we have survived through adaptation, another species will perish because its destiny is tied to continuity and not adaptation.

Our species, the most fragile, the most complex, needs parental protection the longest in nature until it reaches a stage where it can fend for itself. Life is inherently traumatic, and the conditions in which that trauma is absorbed, mediated, or reinforced is a matter of which fated family, which fated environment into which we are thrown. Nature's law is harsh and unforgiving: *that which cannot adapt will perish*. And to what do we adapt? How much of our so-called personality structure, how many of our reflexive strategies, arise out of the traumatic encounter between the child and the incessant demands around them? Who among us here operates out of our natural selves? What forces shaped our readings of the world, and our protective strategies? How amenable are we to change, to replacing some of those adaptations with those more relevant and productive to life's changing conditions? In *Murder in the Cathedral*, T. S. Eliot notes that in a world of fugitives, the person going the right direction will appear to be running away. Who are we, *inherently*, and who are we, *adaptively*?

In my years of analysis in Zürich, and the years since, the thing that I most had to face, and found most difficult to accept, was that what I had become was now my greatest obstacle. What I had become, what we all become, is a series of respondings. A concatenation of colliding causalities leads us to our choices, persists in doing so, and creates our histories and our patterns. One of the most poignant of examples was the testimony of a Victorian era woman who wrote in her diary after her husband's passing that both his life, and hers, had become "a series of respondings." Her husband, Edward, had served as the Archbishop of Canterbury, and now that he was gone, she had no sense of her own identity, so strong had been her capacity to adapt. She felt herself only a broken string of pearls, and she ends the passage by praying to her God to now give her a personality of her own. While the example seems extreme, history is full of such reports, and you may only look around to see contemporary examples. Who would we be without certain conditions obliging certain adaptations and producing certain patterns which over time grow locked in.

When folks have asked me through the years where to start in one's own self-analysis, I have usually said, "Start with your patterns, especially those you find troubling, perhaps self-defeating, injurious to self or others. We do not do crazy things; we always act logically if we understand the intra-psychic premise, or 'idea,' that has been activated." While we can't talk about the unconscious directly, we can take these patterns and work backwards to assemble a pretty good idea of what "idea" or premise has been triggered within us. At the end of that silken thread snaking through the thickets of our psychological history, there is a complex, an affect-laden script with a behavior attached. When catalyzed, it enacts its script, and the attached behavior enters the world. In time, these mechanisms become behavioral patterns, and even when brought to our awareness, we may rationalize them and simply say, "O that's just who I am," or "I have always been that way." Seldom do we surmise that what we are witnessing, and perhaps ratifying, is the relatively arbitrary presence of history, and our adaptations to it in action.

Little do we know that the behavior that just emerged from us—an aggressive response, a flight, an accommodation—had its origin decades ago. We may ask, "Why did I act that way yesterday? What came over me?" Seldom do we tumble to the fact that today's act may very well have its genesis in a time and place before any capacity to reflect upon it or choose differently. No wonder patterns accumulate, no wonder consequences pile up, no wonder we sometimes feel ourselves strangers to ourselves. Nor do we imagine that we are prisoners of arbitrary ministries of fate, and the adaptations which life required of us. However, what is most troubling is that the imposition of that historically-generated behavior imposed on each new situation—and every moment in our lives is a radically new situation—

prejudices that moment, constricts our response, and of course tends to bring back the same old, same old. Until we respond to inner demands for growth, or the challenges of new experiences, including learning as we are attempting here, we are unlikely to break the hold that pattern has upon us. No wonder so often we feel "stuck," burned out, adrift, bored. Desuetude is the loss of directing energy, and when we are in the grip of this history and its adaptive patterns we are rudderless, and are carried by the streams of our past. Remember how Scott Fitzgerald ended his *The Great Gatsby* with a sentence that is now on the tombstone he shares in a Rockville, Maryland churchyard with his wife Zelda: "So we beat on, boats against the current, borne back ceaselessly into the past." What a sad, but truthful epitaph.

We all know we have "stuck places." We often lament our dilatory wills to push through them and get unstuck. What we do not know sufficiently, is how deeply imbedded in our history those adaptive responses are buried, and that they are there to protect us and to manage our anxiety. What would you do without your protections, your anxiety unmanaged? You would be wholly at the mercy of the threats imminent in this world. But what protected us is now a limitation as well, what adapted once now prejudices our possible new moments, what served then now anchors us to a disempowered past. Given that so many of these behaviors arose out of the vulnerable child's limited capacity for action, and limited resources, we can see how often our stuck places take us back to earlier times and undermine, sabotage the adult's much larger resilience and range of behaviors in the present. Given that getting unstuck will automatically elevate our anxiety levels, we see why we rationalize, repeat, and remain stuck. Where so ever a stuck place abides, thereunto an invisible wire reaches into the deeper regions of the person's psychological history. If the person moves against that stuck place, the wiring is activated; a quick current passes along the thread, and the archaic anxiety against which it is defending is activated. Thus, the adaptation that once protected the fragile parts of our lives, again keeps us rooted in the same old rut. In certain parts of the West, we can still see the ruts of the old wagon trains that headed West and Northwest toward California and the Oregon Territory. We have such similar ruts in our psychic life which grow deeper with each repetition of the protective adaptation. This is why change, growth, individuation is so difficult. All require our leaving some seeming safe place for some place more exposed. No wonder we often stay stuck.

Part of the problem of change of course is found in the ready recrudescence of that past with its attendant archaic Angst. But we forget that in the meantime another person has entered our lives, a person with reason, common sense, life experience, many more operational choices, and most of all an inner resilience unknown to the child. That person is also us. Both ordinary maturation and necessity often lift us out of the miasmic past into a more empowered present. But all of us retain swampland areas of vulnerability. First of all, the archaic features of the protective complexes almost always "catastrophize" and produce worst-case outcomes before our mind's eye. For example, "If I speak up," a perilous prospect in some childhoods, now catastrophizes unconsciously as "my partner will leave me forever," or some such. Or, "If I am forthright, I will suffer the incursive wrath of the other, a prospect I can't manage." In most cases, the worst will not happen. And were it to happen the native or acquired resilience we have gained as adults will carry us through to the other side. Only in this shift from the child's perspective, only this move from the marshy swamp of developmental trauma to the ordinary knocks of life can we ever free ourselves, get unstuck. As Freud put it once at the end of a lecture, our task is to move from neurotic misery to the normal misery of life. Even as Lewis Carroll reminded, "We are but children, dear, / who fret to find our bedtimes near." When we can make this move, we are now adults, namely, big people who can manage the normal miseries of life.

As an illustration of this vast assemblage of protective mechanisms we acquire in growing up, consider the following chart:

Existential Adaptive Patterns

I. *Overwhelmment*

A. *Avoidance*: simple avoidance, procrastination, suppression, repression, projection onto others, numbing, distraction, dissociation.
(Personality disorders: avoidant, schizoid, schizotypal)

B. *Power complex*: exercise power over the other by brute force, controlling behaviors, manipulation, passive-aggressive.
Benign complex expresses itself through learning, growth, and greater management of one's life.
(Personality disorders: anti-social {sociopath}, obsessive-compulsive)

C. *Compliance*: give the world what it wants, "to get along, go along"
(Personality disorders: dependent personality, co-dependence)

II. *Abandonment*

A. *Identification with deficit*, substantial wound to self-esteem
   1. Self-sabotage, avoidance, self-denigrative behaviors
   2. Over-compensation by grandiosity
   (Personality disorder: paranoid)

B. *Power Complex*: Use others for narcissistic self-aggrandizement
(Personality disorders: narcissistic personality, histrionic)

C. Inordinate need for self-assurance, excessive neediness.
(Personality disorder: borderline)

Existential philosopher Martin Heidegger said we are "thrown into life," (*geworfen*). So we arrive, naked, alone, at the mercy of whatever the gods have placed in our way. Needing protection until we are able to fend for our own, find our way, absorb the blows that will befall each of us, we have two categorical threats to our survival and well-being: *Overwhelmment* and *Abandonment*. Throughout our lives, they will remain threats and often become tyrants because they dictate our choices, create our patterns, infect our relationships. With notable exceptions, many of the strategies we devise to adapt and protect ourselves as children are still present in later decades, and by now have fixed roles in our on-going coping strategies. One might consider these seemingly necessary protections as something institutionalized within us, or perhaps call them "Shadow Governments," for that is what they do: they govern our lives until we reach sufficient consciousness, and emotional strength, to break their death grip upon our souls.

Overwhelmment

One life message each of us has in common is this: "The world is big, and you are not. The world is powerful, and you are not. Now figure out a way to manage things in the face of that existential discrepancy for the next few decades."The limitations of our capacities may circumscribe our choices, but the range of our adaptabilities creates an almost infinite range of possible strategies. In the engagement with the inherent and inevitable traumata of overwhelmment, we have three basic options:*avoidance, compliance*, and *seizing power* if possible.

Our first, and most primitive defense is avoidance, and oh do we find ways to avoid whatever threats our sensitive warning systems perceive as present. First, and most primitive of all, is simple *avoidance*. The most primitive of primitive defenses is *denial*. What I do not acknowledge is not there, won't happen, is not a threat. I put my fingers in my ears; I close my eyes, and I don't go to the doctor and hear bad news until I am compelled. Behind denial is *simple avoidance*. Step out of harm's way. Avoid that kid on the playground. Don't take that calculus class if you can find a way around it. Rather early in our formative years we learn *procrastination*. We put off our homework, delay our tax preparation, and we hope the problem will go away or magically be solved. We gain some relief from stress by *suppression*. We buy time, plan to deal with it later. Sometimes suppression is necessary so that we can deal with more pressing issues. ("I will silo this, put it away till next week, because I have this matter to contend with first.) Suppression is conscious, willful, and we know we are attempting a sleight of hand while doing it. *Repression*, upon which Freud and Breuer spent so much time, and told us so much, is an unconscious pushing under of the imminent disturbance. We push it into the unconscious. But it doesn't go away. It always goes somewhere. It slides off into the body and becomes a psychosomatic disturbance. It leaks out in slips of the tongue, forgetfulness, camouflaged motives, or troubling dreams. Freud called this "the return of the repressed." And the repressed, like a slain monster in Act II, always returns for its moment of truth in Act III in our lives.

We can disown what is contradictory to our values, or threatening to our ego ideals, by projecting our disowned qualities and motives onto others. "Yon Cassius hath a lean and hungry look. Such men are dangerous." And so we disown our own dark agendas. Jung wrote so eloquently about the Shadow, those parts of our personalities or our groups which, when brought to consciousness we find troubling, contradictory to what we wish, and we dispose of them by way of *projection* onto others. I can see the mote in your eye and miss the log in my own, Jesus noted. In its collective form, this projective disowning results in bigotry, racism, sexism, and most of the violence of our troubled history. Only when the otherness of the Other wears through our projection do we have a chance to see them as they are: a fellow human being, or a person perhaps less awful than we. Shadow work is rare because it asks us to become conscious of what we wish to avoid, and therefore so seldom are shadow projections examined. Our country is riven with Shadow projections these days, always has been, and it is very difficult to find a middle ground in which we can meet our adversaries and experience them as they are, not what our disowned Shadow makes of them. Since projections begin as unconscious protections, I may more likely remain stuck in the morass of ignorance, and find it more comfortable there than in the recognizing the reprehensible in myself as well.

When we reflect on our ailments and disorders, and what our popular culture may do to address them, we find that the chief contribution of modern pop culture is creating a din, a noisy *distracting, numbing* din. Everywhere we turn, we are bombarded by noise, by shiny new things, and by an incalculable number of appeals to purchase something, anything. Today people count their friends though a number on their social medium; their values float like pollen in the sky that is drawn to the nearest sweet place; their philosophy is guided by such sages as the Kardashians, and other celebrities such as Paris Hilton who once expressed her hope that there was an afterlife for if there wasn't, it was all going to be really, really boring. (Celebrities are folks known for being known. They need not have accomplished anything beyond a callipygean butt, nor do they need have anything life-giving to share.) If the anodyne for our distresses is distraction and numbing, what is it that we so have to avoid? Is it not an engagement with the existential questions that persist: *who* am I, *why* am I, *what* am I to do with this life, and so on. If Socrates, who said the unexamined life is not worth living, is right, what are we to make of so many souls on this earth who never reflect on the questions which bring savor and summons to our lives? And what are we to do with a culture that makes it so easy for the soul to slumber on? Such a culture is iatrogenic; it is part of the problem.

Lastly, among the strategies of avoidance, is *dissociation*. In the extreme forms of avoidance of the pressures of this moment we observe the dissociative identity disorder. In truly traumatic circumstances, as colleague Don Kalsched has pointed out, this extreme measure demonstrates how the Self ingeniously contrives a way for the psyche to survive. Sooner or later, whatever we avoid will show up on our doorstep. Jung put it so eloquently when he said, what we avoid within will have a propensity for showing up in our lives and we will call it *Fate*. But we will have played an unwitting role in the fomenting of that fate.

The next line of defense after avoidance is *compliance* with the pressures of the Other. "To get along you go along." "Give them what they want and they will leave you alone." These are things we tell ourselves. The message of childhood dependence, very real, daily reinforced, is over-learned. It tends to infantilize people. It tells folks to turn to some big person to tell them what to do, or better, take care of the problem for us. Few of us wish to admit to dependencies, but they show up in moments of crisis, testing, defeat, loss, and disappointment. Far more of us are willing to acknowledge some measure of what we today call *co-dependence*. In the co-dependent's daily log book, the Other is almost always more powerful. The Other will be upset with us if we don't comply. The Other is more entitled to something than we are. And besides, we are not dependent people, are we? Co-dependence is another legacy of our earliest messages of the power of the world around us, and our vulnerability to that power.

In time, the co-dependent person tends to lose contact with the wisdom and guidance of the Self; at worst, they become psychological chameleons, taking on the coloration of the environment in which they find themselves. For a brief while, the American Psychiatric Association considered including co-dependence in the *Diagnostic and Statistical Manual*—the Bible of contemporary diagnosis. But insurance companies lobbied against this inclusion, as if they should even be at the table for such an important consideration, and the APA abandoned the idea because any diagnosis that included the great majority of a culture could hardly then be called a disorder, a pathology. Recovering from co-dependence is extremely difficult because of its reflexive response to the stimuli. But we all have to make an effort to pull back from reflexive responses, consult our legitimate feelings and perspectives on matters, and perhaps decide based on legitimate self-interest. This is why I sometimes call myself "a recovering Nice Guy." We were all raised to be nice, really nice. A reflexive "niceness" is a pathogenic loss of connection to the soul, and is not nice. The opposite of such a reflexive niceness is called authenticity, or integrity.

The third categorical response to the largeness of the world around us, and to our vulnerability to it, requires the acquisition of *power*. In its crudest form you see people murder others who don't comply. Inside each dictator is a frightened, abused child who is driven to over-compensation. But we all have moments when the power complex grabs hold of us and makes us do things we later regret, if we ever bother to reflect and count costs. What relationship is power-free? Power itself is not the problem. Power is the energy needed to address life's tasks. Power caught in a complex can be blind, unreasoning, violent, and non-reflective. Wherever we feel weakest, most vulnerable, most embarrassed is where the power complex is most likely to emerge. If the person feels disempowered, then she or he can turn to passive-aggressive strategies. One exerts control over the other through subtle sabotages. We don't carry through on a commitment; we arrive late; we undermine the situation, and so on. Passive-aggressive behavior is still aggressive. It is the power of the powerless, and is sometimes just as deadly.

Of course there are benign forms of the power complex such as this present moment of dialogue as we try to learn from each other. We have education; we have travel; we have reservoirs of information available, and so on—all designed to help us clear a space for ourselves in this troubled transit we call our life. Tools such as will, meditation, dream work, seminars and classes, books, and so on are all avenues for the constructive access to power.

Each of these strategies—*avoidance, compliance, power*—will show up in each of our lives from time to time. In fact, we need to see all of these patterns operating somewhere in our lives. And relatively healthy folks can step back and see these behaviors and correct or modify them. They are the "healthy neurotic." There are those who through extreme biochemical inheritance, or more commonly invasive traumatic experience, have no choice but to serve those de facto strategies. These are what we call the "personality disorders" and are extremely resistant to treatment and modification. It is as if the core program guiding this person's life is the strategy, the protection, and no deviation from its iron grip is tenable.

Abandonment

The other existential threat is *abandonment*. In our most vulnerable beginnings, without the protection and nurturance of the Other, we would all perish. Even in later life, radical abandonment, as in cases of solitary confinement, can produce "anaclitic depression." We are social animals, and without the other, without touch, some kind of intra-human engagement, our systems shut down, leading to immobilization, opportunistic illnesses, and a sickness of the soul. It may be argued that our agenda of needs from the Other will always be short-changed, and that some part of each of us will always feel forlorn and lost. Most of us, most of the time, can manage to keep ourselves together. The recent pandemic has certainly pushed many folks to the limit in their isolation. Several nations now have cabinet level positions staffed with persons in charge of a portfolio addressing rampant loneliness in our mass society. But for the great majority of us, just as there were three basic responses to the threat of overwhelmment, so there are three categories of response to the insufficiencies of our nurturant environments.

It is the nature of our subjective reactions to our fated circumstances that we all—children, adults, those under stress—engage in "magical thinking," the tendency to explain the outer world by reference to our inner psychic state at the time. Accordingly, it often leads a child to conclude, and sometimes even the adult in later years, that "I am what happened to me." Rather than see ourselves as inherent, self-directing organisms, we internalize such conditions as sterile family environments, invasive emotional atmospheres, drug and alcohol environments, deleterious social conditions, even the effect of the Zeitgeist as a statement to us about us. My parents grew up in poverty, and I in lean times, so one of the ontological beliefs engendered by this environment was a conviction of inherent deficiency, a lack of expectation for anything better, and a tendency to not ask for anything or feel entitled to anything larger. (That reminds me of the old joke, "I have always had an inferiority complex, but it is not a very good one.") All of us, somewhere in our history, have experienced insufficiency and therefore internalized that sense of deficit as a telling aspect of ourselves.

Accordingly, the first aspect of the response to abandonment is to identify with insufficiency: "The world is not enough. It's never enough, and therefore I am not enough." Naturally, this presumption leads to *wounds to self-esteem* which are so common to our species. Out of that diminishment of one's being two opposing patterns evolve. The first, and most common, leads to *self-sabotage, avoidance of risk and opportunity, self-denigrative behaviors.* How many of us do not feel a core "permission" to have our lives, to feel what we feel, desire what we desire, and the permission to pursue them at all costs in the world around us? How many times have we shot ourselves in the foot? How often do we look at decisive junctures in our life and see we did not elect the road less traveled? How many days does coulda-woulda-shoulda show up in our lives? Remember, our life may objectively be rich with opportunities; and we may have talents, interests, enthusiasms untapped, but we settle for the same old, same old. Generally, the old, old premise is hard to dislodge, and we learn to grow content, even love our limitations for they are, in their protective way, familiar and spare us the risk of genuine trial in this world. We spend our days breathing in constricted chambers; they are our psychic prisons.

Concomitantly, the reverse strategy rises: we tend to *over-compensate by attaining outer accoutrements of power, success, achievement*: "Look at my house, look at my bright, shiny children, look at my status symbols out in my front yard." Such persons are always haunted by the threat of inadequacy, feelings of fraud. They fear that one fine day the committee will show at the front door and proclaim to the world their insufficiencies. Soon, "they will find me out. I guess I will have to work harder to attain more of those symbols of power and success. But when will it ever be enough to feel ok about me?" The answer of course is never. For, as the witticism attributed to Pearl Bailey says, "Thems what thinks they is, ain't."

Second is the *inordinate need for reassurance from others, or excessive neediness*. Needfulness is human for none of us is wholly adequate to the crushing panoply of life's demands. But neediness drives folks away from us. We have all met people who keep wanting something from us, and that pressure in time pushes us away, and they are left with a familiar empty-handedness. The critical word here is *inordinate*, or excessive. Where is that fine line between asking for help in this difficult journey, and when it is really up to us to figure it out? In the book on relationships I called *The Eden Project*, I noted that there is an heroic question each of us is called to address in all our relationships, ranging from intimacy to our relationship to the collective society itself. That question is *"What do I need to address myself in order not to lay that burden on another?"* I call this heuristic question "heroic" because it asks us to step into the field of hero energy in our life journey, be responsible, and take on the individuation project for ourselves. It is also a loving thing to do, for it frees others, our partners, our children, our comrades from the burdens of our life so they can tend more adequately to theirs.

The third pattern in our response to insufficiency is our old friend again, *the power complex*. We all have narcissistic wounds, that is, wounds to our core sense of self. And if we're lucky to have doting parents, life will still kick us in the teeth somewhere down the line; fate will someday shove us to the side of the road. If that hasn't yet happened, one's turn will eventually come. This is why in all of us there are behaviors, both unconsciously and consciously manipulative, that are in service to narcissistic self-aggrandizement. The more intimate the relationship, the more likely we are to replicate some of life's early deficits, and the more subtle the power stratagems that slide below the surface of our relationships. This is why "the heroic question" I just mentioned is always relevant to us.

While we all have narcissistic wounds, we need not be full blown narcissists. Contrary to the classical etiology of Narcissus, the Greek youth who fell in love with his own Selfie in the pool, the true narcissist stares in the mirror and no one stares back. That is why she or he must use others to counter their sense of emptiness. The old joke about the narcissist is "Well now…enough about me. What do you think about me?" The narcissist's wound is never filled; it is an abyss. "What have you done for me lately?" If the narcissist is the boss, or a parent, those in the field of its influence will never receive genuine reciprocity or caring in return. The true narcissist will remind us of the size of his crowds, or name buildings after himself, or use others and throw them away. But his or her journey is desolate, and ends always in emptiness.

Each of us needs to see all six of these reactive patterns as adaptive measures, necessary and protective in our past, and playing a role of varying influence in our current lives. (Briefly, they are the following: avoidance, compliance, power, and an internalized identification of deficit, power, and inordinate neediness.) If you do not, that missing pattern is unfolding through you unconsciously. Don't dare ask others how they experience being around you if you don't want to hear about it.

We can now see, but must not judge, each of these reflexive adaptive systems in our lives, systems that become autonomous governance agencies that make decisions for us, and create our patterns, and replicate consequences for good or ill. We all squander these precious hours we are granted in wallows of stuckness. I literally recommend that one photo-copy this schema of *Existential Adaptive Patterns*, tape it to a place where you will see it every day, and review it often enough to begin catching these invisible governments in our lives. We don't do crazy things; we do logical things, if we understand the historic premises triggered. Seeing a pattern allows us to say, for example, "That behavior of mine is coming out of an experience of powerlessness in this relationship. Am I in fact powerless? What can I, as an adult, do differently; how may I draw upon my richer present and richer armamentarium of actions than the child had?"

In the training of Zen practitioners, novices are presented with a Koan, a riddle or paradoxical dilemma with no rational answer. Its purpose is to confound the ego with its familiar framing devices, and occasion a renewed encounter with the primacy of present, felt experience. The Zen-like paradox of our lives is that what we became, perhaps *had* to become, is now the chief obstacle to a larger life, a more capacious journey. Those very adaptations, defenses, archaic accommodations, now bind us to the limitations of our past. Something has to jar us loose from those historic shackles and pull us into a felt encounter with the radical presence of this moment. Only in this way can we begin to reclaim our lives from history. Only in this way can we begin to break through into the growth that the soul is asking of us. Only in this kind of move may the spirit, allied with an aroused consciousness, work in partnership and step more fully into our journey. Only in this way can I be an adult, something more than having a big body or a big role in life. Only in this way can I begin to serve something larger than my fears. Only in this way can I share the journey of Tennyson's Ulysses who reminds all of us, "tis not too late to seek a newer world.... Some work of noble note may yet be done, / not unbecoming [those] who strove with gods." Only in this way can our world be made new.

CHAPTER THREE

Necessary Fictions: Therapy as the Critique of "Stories"

We are creatures who need to understand, at any cost. And so we "story" our experiences, and those stories—provisional, localized, and often created at an early stage of our history—become defining narratives. The disarray of our histories nevertheless can be a powerful clue to the "meta-stories" to which we have been in service for many years. Therapy can be understood as the identification of and critical analysis of our operative or "meta-stories." Until these "narrative interpretations" can be smoked out, we remain their captive. In a series of questions, we will be invited to examine the stories we have been serving, and then engage stories that honor what wants to unfold from within us.

> "We tell ourselves stories in order to live."
> Joan Didion

We have talked about the gift of adaptation to help us, in our helpless states, survive and find a living space. We have also talked about the contentious atmosphere within most of us most of the time, the conflict between the understandable desire for safety, satiety, and surcease of tensions, even as the omnipresent challenges of life compel our responses. Wedged forever in between these energy systems, the need for survival and the ambivalence with which we encounter life's demands, something peculiar, and definitive, emerges. All animals learn reflexive responses to stress, hunger, danger and desire, but this particular animal who evolved as an amalgam of the surging sea and the shifting sands—made still mostly of water, and adorned by fleeting fabrics of humus—brings a different dimension. This animal is a story-telling, story-creating beast. Our animal kin live mostly by response to the surge of instinct within, but we peculiar creatures create narratives about it all. Sometimes our narratives address questions important in our search for origins; sometimes they help us bear the weight of suffering better; sometimes they help us live in harmony with the world around us; and sometimes the same stories imprison us within the confines of their mythy motions. An old Hebraic legend has it that God created humans to have someone to share stories with. And there are those, of course, who think the gods are themselves but a story, a more appealing story perhaps than the thought of living in an empty, and drafty, apartment house.

While our stories may acquire an aesthetic dimension, their first and primal task is to feed us information that serves survival. When a child first touches the hot iron, it has thereafter a story to mark the moment, a story that follows and protects. But what if that story also extends to other, similar shiny objects with cords? Then the same protective story can quickly constrict. One of our human tendencies is to confabulate, to extend our stories as far afield as possible in order to milk further utility from them. Soon, those stories begin to make judgements that dictate behaviors, and create hierarchies of value. What begins as a need to understand, to make sense of raw experience, may over time become phobias, ideologies, causes, scripts, and even personal scriptures. Consider this example. When my daughter Taryn was a toddler, we attended an end of the year picnic at the university president's home. She was drawn toward a big, wooly English sheepdog, and he to her. With her legs unsteady, she was nudged by him over a hillock, where he playfully followed her, jumping on her on the way down. On the way to the bottom of the incline, she evolved a different story. She was being devoured by a huge white monster. Around the same time, she was stung by some insect, which we generically named a "bee." For a while, these two stories merged in her infant imagination. All animals were labeled "bees"; all were threats, and all triggered moments of terror. Even a neighbor's dog was enough to produce a mini-panic attack. The *phenomenon* was her encounter with nature at play; the *epiphenomenon* was the story that helped a child make some sense of her trauma. Finally, we bought a small white dog about the size of an adult shoe, clearly in the toy category rather than monster category, and as the dog grew, another story emerged alongside the first. Both stories remain inside, for nothing that ever happened to us is wholly effaced. Either one, theoretically, may be evoked in any moment. Apart from the natural maturation process that moved her into a big body and a person with considerable resources, these two stories may still contend. Yet, living now just north of Dallas, my dear daughter has three dogs. We can see which of these stories helped recontextualize the primitive phenomena and prevailed. But finding a larger story is not always the outcome. More often, the ancient, archaic stories continue their versions of the world, and become our adaptive realties. So it is with all of us; at all times, we are a congeries of stories, interpretations, epiphenomenal renderings of raw experience into narrative form in the hope of understanding it.

My deceased son, Timothy, once emailed me a poem titled "Facing Self" in which he conjured with the "idea" of our stories. The last two stanzas show his comfort in employing these stories as useful fictions, that is, stories not to be taken literally but which nonetheless illumine us more than the mysteries in which we swim.

Our ideas of perfection-
curse words overheard, kindness overlooked,
or our magazines and neighbors-
are just as absurd as the idea
that we have what it takes
to make God happy
or that God wants.

Does God want
as much as we?
History has shown me the psychopath, and
the monk who alights himself for peace;
and is it any God that wants
anything more
than a beautiful kiss
that I think
even the worst sinner has experienced?
at least once?

One senses that Tim was not captivated by his stories, but was consciously toying with them with both a touch of humor and deadly seriousness. He was aware of the fictive nature of all our utterances. When we use the word *fiction* or *fictive*, we do not mean "falsehood." Quite the contrary, fiction comes from the Latin *facere*, "to make," from which we get also *fabric* and *factory*, places where things are made. Fictions are tools we have found to help us stand in relationship to all that which is ultimately inexplicable. As such, the tools may immensely help us approach the unapproachable, but beware the danger to those who forget the origin of their fictions. Humans are known for falling in love with their own constructs, for being captivated by their own metaphors. History is replete with ravening blood lust in service to the superiority of "our" story over that of our neighbor. No army, I believe, has ever marched off to war singing, "Our metaphor is better than yours; our fiction more useful than yours."

Forgetting the origins of our fictions creates real prisons. I recall once giving a talk on behalf of the National Endowment for the Humanities in Arkansas in 1973 in which I was illustrating how scholars might help a person today understand what the unknown author of the book of John might have meant in that opening sentence: "In the beginning was the word, and the word was with God, and the word was God." An agitated lady explained to the audience, and the stupid visiting speaker, that her brother was a student of the Bible and always said that one should not change one word in any way from what God had directly written. I asked her if her brother spoke any of the dialects of Aramaic, the language Jesus would have spoken, or Greek in which this text was written. She quickly retorted that those notables, Jesus and God, both spoke English as any fool could read for himself. Well, this fool moved on with the talk as soon as he could.

Linked to our survival, and adaptation agenda, we "story" our environment, and the events that transpire therein. This "storying" is both a curious and an anxiety-driven stratagem to make as much sense of the inexplicable as we can. In ca. 1800, Immanuel Kant reminded us that we never know the

Ding an Sich, the "thing in itself," but rather the experience of our subjective renderings of it. Since each of us has a different subjective terrain, a different series of histories with their imposing analogical templates, our "stories" about the same event will often vary so greatly. (Think of the number of stories witnesses provide after observing a traumatic event.) All of us have had the experience of returning to a former locale in our history, perhaps to that once cavernous grade school in which the desks and even the teachers now seem so tiny. They were not tiny then, as our stories so often reflect. In the nineteenth century because of the progressive erosion of the fixity of the "object," that is, the presumption of the immutable, solid, knowable Other, we see the movement from realism to impressionism to expressionism to Dadaism to abstract art. We also had to "invent" phenomenology and depth psychology to study, if not the fading object, then our subjective tools for rendering a story around it.

The French poet Guillaume Apollinaire once wrote in *Cors de Chasse* that memory is a hunting horn whose sound fades along the wind. So, we find so many false, distorting memories. We may swear that something happened just this way, and then find a very plausible account that completely revisions the event. Given that we "story" our lives constantly, we can so easily become prisoners not of what happened but our subjective renderings, our stories of what happened. At best our stories are subjective, provisional, localized, and the most formative and persistent are likely those which we created in our beginnings. From infancy onward, we are interpreting our experience. The survival and well-being of a child depends on her or his asking such questions as:"Is the Other stable, trustworthy, reliable, or the reverse?" Naturally, the child's sample is very limited, but such a story, that is to say interpretive narrative, is the only game in town, and will inevitably show up in relationships decades later. Consider that question one of many that establishes a set of provisional assumptions in its critical query: consider others, such as: "Do I have the right to ask for what I need, or does that make things worse?" "Do I have permission to express my reality, or must it be leveraged against each new *Sitz im Leben* to ascertain whether it will be safe, acceptable or not?" "And what about me? Am I, as I am, acceptable? Or do I have to twist and torque myself into some shape that will be safe, even loved?" The provisional, tentative, and often infantile reading of the world, and the stories that rise from those encounters tend to generate an entire operating system that governs a person's life, what I call a meta-story, a story about our stories. No matter how conscious or mature a person may be, she or he will always find contemporary decisions, reactions, expectations to be strained through the alembic of our historic narratives. To ignore this profound influence, this prejudicing of the present, is to remain a captive of history. No matter how tall the skyscraper, the elevator always goes through the bottom floors first. How much we are free, in any given present moment, and how much we are looking at the world through the distorting lens of our fictive renderings is a perplexing but potentially perspicacious paradox. Thus, one might say, a rigorous therapy might be defined as an on-going critique of our narrative structures.[11]

Through the years, the most useful, most pragmatic on a daily level, of Jung's concepts is that of the *complex.* While he did not coin the term, he made it his to explain how any triggering moment in our outer lives can catalyze a splinter of our history. All of our experiences register the amount of energy, trauma, significance of any given moment, and that

---

[11] Remember the old saying, "Gossip is living history. History is petrified gossip."

cluster of energy not only has its program to play out, but it always manifests in our bodies, and presents us with a de facto lens through which to see this new, unique in history moment. This is a profound discovery, or articulation from a scientific basis, of what all generations have recognized in their folk wisdom. "Write the letter but don't send it for a few days. See if you feel the same way then." Or, "Count to twenty before you reply." Long has humanity recognized the spectral energy that passes over us, possesses us for a short while, and then recedes back into the unconscious. Even our "contemporary" Hamlet could make conscious such autonomous presences within him when he described how "resolution is sicklied over with the pale cast of thought and loses the name of action." What a perfect description of being seized by a complex. "The pale cast of thought"... do we even know it is happening? And do we recognize it has substituted its old, old template for our present adult spectrum of possible responses? As Kant noted, when you wear blue spectacles, you will see a blue world with only blue choices available.

The Greek imagination similarly intuited the presence of these internal "stories," scripts, distorting lenses. What we call the tragic vision dramatized the work of these invisible powers in the construction of our lives and their outcomes. Fate (*moira*) limits, and directs us. Destiny (*proeiroismus*) tugs us into ever-larger futures. But we see through the *hamartia*, what I would call "the distorting lens." How often in the moment whatever we choose may well rise from seeing the present through the lens of our family of origin, or our religious or cultural conditioning. The ancients were right to ask if freedom is even possible for humans, given the force fields at work in us in any given moment. Invariably, the tragic protagonist is in trouble the moment she or he goes down one path or another, having made the choice in the full flush of an assumption that such an option is the exercise of conscious, free will. It is this presumption that leads to the unraveling of events. Henceforth, the only appropriate attitude is humility, to know that one does not know, to remember that in the moment of hybristic inflation, the gods are watching. In the Bible, this is what is meant by the admonition of "go in fear of the Lord." The "fear" is not intimidation by some cosmic bully but a reminder of how seductive it is to think we always know enough to know enough, when in truth we never know enough to know enough, even as action is required from us. Rather, the thing to fear is presumptive "certainty," inflation.

From such complex intra-psychic machinery, we build a life. I feel obliged to repeat Jung's caution that whatever is denied inwardly will have a tendency to come to us in the outer world, although we will then think it the act of fate. Were we to visualize our histories, we would see swirling clusters of energy, multi-colored streams flowing through any moment, disappearing, reappearing elsewhere. Impossible as it is to visualize this flow of psychic energies as a painter might, depth psychology is tasked with that burden of discernment. The very disarray of our histories, the repetitive compulsions as Freud called them, the dammed-up places, the open wounds which spatter this hour, and the people around us—all this can be a powerful guide to the "stories" to which we have been in service for many years. How can we know what is unconscious until it invests itself in an image? Once the image is present—in a bodily state, a dream drama, a behavioral pattern—then we have a shot at getting into that invisible world. Until we smoke these stories out, we are doomed to repeat them.

Typically, in and of our lives, or the lives of others, we have conscious stories, what we tell ourselves on a daily basis. But there are always other stories afoot. I was shocked when I opened a photo album left behind by my deceased mother. In it, she had written a note by a photo of the two of us, perhaps when I was about six or so. I remember most of those years as troubled times, years when we all sought to discern what mood was afoot and to avoid it or fix it. In her note, she wrote, "Jimmy was always trying to make his mother laugh." While I was glad that she remembered it that way, and no doubt her note was true enough, I also wondered if that did not reveal something about the child's experience being "storied" very early, that his best bet was to try to inject humor to lighten the moment. Though I don't want to make too much of that particular photo, that, allied with many other examples, makes one wonder if the seeds of being a "wounded healer" were not only planted that early but already calling the shots. If that were true, *if*....then how much freedom is there in a choice of vocation such as the one I have?

Poet Naomi Replansky writes in her poem "An Inheritance,"

"Five dollars, four dollars, three dollars, two,
One, and none, and what do we do?"

This is the worry that never got said
But ran so often in my mother's head

And showed so plain in my father's frown
That to us kids it drifted down.

It drifted down like soot, like snow,
In the dream-tossed Bronx, in the long ago.

I shook it off with a shake of the head.
I bounced my ball, I ate warm bread,

I skated down the steepest hill.
But I must have listened, against my will:

When the wind blows wrong, I can hear it today.
Then my mother's worry stops all play

And, as if in its rightful place,
My father's frown divides my face.[12]

Many of us probably grew up with money worries in the family, or health issues, or substance abuse, and whatever the prevailing atmosphere construed, so we were "storied" by our experience of it. Just as sprayed shrapnel causes wounds to bleed, these invisible energy dispersals flush through us and we bleed invisibly. Years later, when things are going well there is a part of one's psyche held back, waiting for the blow, waiting for the proverbial shoe to drop. Natural enthusiasm, the ability to enjoy oneself, be spontaneous—all may be curbed, even excluded by such a story as it serves as the filter through which the present moment must always pass. Remember that Jung reminded us, we cannot solve such "meta-stories," but we can outgrow them. It is especially difficult to outgrow them if we do not even know how they cast a hue over the world as we see it. Until these "narrative interpretations" can be smoked out, we remain their captive. Until then, we live, as Shakespeare writes in Sonnet 111, such that our "nature is subdued/ to what it works in, like the dyer's hand."

---

[12] https://poets.org/poem/inheritance-1

While there are stories we tell ourselves, there are also stories which "tell us," though we know it not. The power of such stories rises from our over-identification with what happened to us. Given such messages, we often ratify this fallacy of over-generalization, and thus repeat and reinforce their lodging in our psychic houses. In so many households, the children scatter like spilled seeds into their separate futures. One will remain the unseen child, even when she is half a century old; one will be the fixer, and will be cursed with an inability to say no to the needs of others; one will be a scapegoat, and make redundant choices which sabotage and confirm this role. Similarly, cultural atmospheres such as gender roles and constrictions, racial, ethnic, and economic categories—all may grind that lens through which one sees the spectra of choices open to the adult. One child will be compelled to repeat its message in the next generation; one will be driven to "anything but that," and still be owned by "that"; and one will be out there trying to fix or heal it through a life of distraction, narcosis, or perhaps discovering its compelling power through therapy.

Freud provided us an early topographic survey of how we deal with such stories, whether we know their presence or not: repression, projection on to others, splitting, and so on. Our stories incarnate over and over through our daily history. Seeking to read that history tips us to the notion that there might be such invisible agents at work within us. Then we may at last begin to access the movement of the invisible fields of energy through the visible world of choice, consequence and pattern.

Internal crises of identity, or role, or exhaustion of resources or an antiquated story, or the intervention of others...whatever, sometimes allows us to begin to ask such questions as: *Who am I, apart from my history? What does my history make me do, or keep me from doing? When I make one of those critical choices at a juncture in life, what is that really in service to inside me?* And, occasionally, we may even ask the question: *What wants to enter the world through me?* This latter question is a movement beyond the iron grip of history into some enlarging service to the summons of individuation. This is the moment when fate can yield to destiny. To bring us to this moment of *metanoia*, or transformation of consciousness, is the task of therapy, or whatever life experience brings us to enlightenment. In those new hours, we will not be spared conflict or struggle of course, but the struggle may prove in service to enlargement rather than diminishment. Jung put it this way, "Individuation...means intense consciousness of conflict. You never will be saved from conflict as long as you live, otherwise you would be dead before you die. Conflict cannot be removed. If it seems to be removed, that is imaginary. Conflict must be, if one lives at all. But the way you deal with it, that is the question—whether you are overcome by the conflict, whether you get drowned in it, whether you get identified with one or the other side of the conflict. Individuation simply means you find your place amid the turmoil; you keep yourself in the midst of the conflict; you are in the conflict yet above it."[13]

Let me give some other examples, beginning with one from my recently deceased friend, the poet Stephen Dunn. Once we had offices next to each other back in academia, and we often talked about his family's influence upon him. As a child he knew that there was a meta-story coursing beneath the surface of daily life, a tension between his father and his

---

[13] C. G. Jung, *Dream Symbols of the Individuation Process*, p.35. Seminar held at Bailey Island, Maine, 1936.

mother which, while omnipresent, was never explained. In a poem titled "Regardless," he recalls the many times he went to fetch his father at the pub, and the frigid silences that pervaded the dinner hour. Once his father took him to see the roiling surf as a hurricane approached the Rockaways. He was thrilled to be with his father, thrilled to see the unfolding of the awesome powers of nature. When they got home, his mother stood waiting, solemnly, and that old atmosphere descended again, now with the added charge of "child endangerment." Stephen concludes his brief tour of childhood, and his encounter with some ominous, recondite story which lurked behind the scenes of those tense dinner hours with the distancing line, "I must have thought damage is just what happens."[14] Think of that sentence—how a child derives from what tools he has at the moment: "damage is just what happens." Damage then, must be the norm, not aberrant, not explicable through information, but apparently just the nature of things. And then, of course, one always has to ask the question, "And how did that reading of events show up in your subsequent life?" Did it make you more sensitive, inured to conflict, avoidant, what? In another poem, he speculates that he learned to engage conflict by armoring himself with silence.

It was only years later that Stephen learned the meta-story behind such hours of troubled weather, outer and inner. His mother's father, his grandfather, lived with them. At some point he had a mistress dying of cancer, and he came to Steve's father and asked for a loan to pay her medical bills. The loan was never repaid, and when Stephen's mother asked for the reason their savings were gone, he replied that he had lost the money at the track. Not

---

[14] Stephen Dunn, "Regardless," *Landscape at the End of the Century*, p. 34.

only had Stephen internalized some meta-story whispering behind the walls, he had always thought of his father as a kind of outcast, someone who was found each morning on the couch having fallen asleep reading Eugene O'Neill or Shakespeare. While the actual story helped him understand the tensions in that house, even more he had to recast his father's life from ne'er-do-well and drunkard to someone who had operated on principle, and bore the brunt of everyone's misunderstanding and estrangement quietly and heroically. Seldom in life do we get to know the actual events from an adult's perspective, and so we are left to construct a narrative from limited information, and from the truncated vision of a child. So it is, we march on into life, doing the best we can, serving the only stories we know, or believe we know.

Years later, Stephen and his wife were living in Spain, and one night a terrible pounding on the tin roof above them woke them in fright. There seemed no storm outside, nor was there a tree branch to lash that surface. Both felt the presence of the uncanny; both thought, against reason, that some spectral presence was seeking admission. The next morning, he received a telegram from New York City that his father had died at that very hour. Years later, he wrote of that night in a poem titled, "My Ghost,"

> An outgoing man, my father once held back
> a truth that could have rescued him from sadness.
> Now he roams the night, my inheritance,
> in every word I hear him speak. He vanishes,
> returns, no place for him in this entire world.[15]

---

[15] Ibid., "My Ghost," *Everything Else in the World*, p. 23.

Stephen concluded, again against common sense, that his father, homeless, was seeking a warm place, a place where he might finally be welcome.

If Stephen's view of his father was tilted by the omnipresence of a story, a false story, his view of his mother generated the sort of meta-story that extrapolates to other women, and was derived from her care and openness to him. He recounts this incident as he made his bumpy way into adolescence with all its daunting challenges.

> when I was twelve,
> 1951, before the world
> unbuttoned its blouse.
>
> I had asked my mother (I was trembling)
> if I could see her breasts
> and she took me into her room
>
> without embarrassment or coyness
> and I stared at them,
> afraid to ask for more.[16]

In this poem Stephen goes on to reflect on how that moment affected his life. His mother's openness and trust in him, he speculates, allowed him to form a story of trust and comfort with women the rest of his life. I, on the other hand, knew full well that had I made a similar request my head would have been on a pike at the end of the driveway before dusk.

My mother was the daughter of a Swedish coal miner who came to this land to find a new life. But early on, the cave he was working in collapsed and killed him when she was a child, and she never got to know him. (This was one of those mines the famed Mother Jones was leading demonstrations against at the time in Illinois and Pennsylvania for their poor

---

[16] Ibid., "The Routine Things Around the House," *Not Dancing*, p. 39.

safety record. And for those who died, there was no gold watch, no insurance, no benefits.) Her mother was a lovely woman with no skills but sewing, so she became a seamstress. Throughout grade school my mother wore dresses made from flour sacks which had patterns on them then. On her text books and school documents an *I* was always stamped. She did not know till much later that *I* meant *Indigent*. She grew up with nothing, and of course internalized, as we saw in the previous grid of existential defense systems, a massive insecurity and inherent unworthiness. You will perhaps believe the two short anecdotes I am about to tell are contrived, ridiculous—but they are facts. And, they are wholly "logical" once one realizes the depth of the premise of her core story, the one that dominated her life because it dominated her childhood. When later, I was on the scene, and she learned that a neighborhood boy was going to get music lessons, and moreover, was known to play tennis, she told me I probably should not play with him anymore. She was not being constrictive; she was being protective. She assumed that anyone who would have access to such middle-class pursuits as music and tennis would surely belong in an atmosphere more rarified than ours. By keeping me away, she sought to spare me such humiliation as she had routinely experienced. That story, the internalization of her life conditions, dominated our family.

During my last conversation with her, when both of us knew she had but a short time to live from cancer, I thought I might please her by telling her that my book *Tracking the Gods* was now translated into Swedish, her father's language, and in fact had been given an award from the Swedish Cultural Ministry. But her response to this news was mortification. She was afraid that, by even writing something, I was now "out there," unprotected, at the mercy of critics, and of course those more entitled people. And of course she was right, but she could not imagine that her son had grown some armor by then, that he was capable of handling reversals, and that he thought maybe sometimes we have to do what we have to do even when we are afraid. That her last hour with me she was caught in the old fearfulness, and the old lack of entitlement to live a free life, still fills me with grief.

These observations naturally lead us to some conclusions which have a certain demand to make of us. When we begin to explore our stories, especially those affecting large decisions in our lives, where do we begin? As I mentioned, even that photograph with my mother caused me, decades later, to reflect on what sort of marching orders I might have received, or concocted on my own, during those early years, and where they may have taken or blocked me later. Sometimes dreams help us challenge our stories. Finding that many folks in later life, myself included, have dreams of people and places left long behind might suggest that our psyche continues to rework this material. Perhaps it is helping us bring to the surface the invisible players, and the ghostly scripts enacted on our inner stages. Other times, we have to examine our patterns, how we reflexively avoid conflict, or try to make nice, or feel riddled with angst from the smallest of provocations. Then we have a clue, an invitation to a forensic exploration of our origins, our primal stories, our operating systems.

We can, and must, do most of this forensic exploration ourselves. We need to ask these questions to stir the pot, to nudge the unconscious to respond.

I know my outer biography, my resume, my life history, but what implicit stories might they be embodying, what meta-stories dictate the contours of my biography?

What sort of premise, interpretation, cluster of history might give rise to the patterns I see, especially those patterns which are counter-productive to me, and perhaps hurtful to others?

What stories might I have received from, or correctives I am implicitly trying to make, to my psychological inheritance? (Jung himself felt obliged to address the questions his extended family of six clerics failed to address regarding the sorry state of the spirit in the modern era.)

What stories might still be seeking to enter the world through me?

What stories ask that I address the questions raised by my unlived life, the one that beckons, perhaps haunts?

What unlived story asks of me courage, submission to something larger than the comforts of the past, and considerable risk-taking?

When we pay attention, we realize that our life is swarming with fragmented stories, multiplicities of splinter narratives contending for our attention, our investment of energy; and coursing beneath all of our acquired stories an even larger story awaits us; it is the story to be served through what Jung described as *individuation*. When we become accountable to this larger story, our life attains high drama each day; each decision stands before the enlargement/diminishment crossroads. Each day brings a new assignment to show up in service to what wishes expression through us. Each hour provides a more conscious set of assignments for us to attend. Then, we find, our life has grown more interesting to us, and invites our co-authorship in its unfolding patterns, its plot twists, and its mysterious assignations with destiny. Each hour, life asks each of us *how* shall you live? *How* shall you die? And will you die before you die? Each hour, our story grows larger, or it grows smaller. So much of our story was written by fate, so much written by others. At least some small part of it, perhaps the best part, is yet to be written by us. And the soul's hour, this hour we inhabit now, asks of us: *And how will you write your story from this hour onward?*

CHAPTER FOUR

Down and Out in Zürich: For Those Who Think Becoming a Jungian Analyst is a Cool Thing

The writer tries to warn those who think becoming a Jungian analyst is a cool thing, a journey of the liberated spirit which transcends the carnage and muck of lived life. He thoughtfully warns you of what you might have to face, and the price you may need to pay. He defeats his purpose, partly against good sense and reason, by giving you a happy ending, and hopes that the reader will not be seduced by that into ignoring the miserable price of the journey, and perhaps also the price of not taking the journey.

Through the years, I have had dozens and dozens of folks approach me in person, or now electronically, and say some version of this, "*I read Memories, Dreams, Reflections*, and I would like to become a Jungian analyst." Or even, "I read your book X, and I would like to become a Jungian analyst." I can understand why folks have that reaction for they have, at least momentarily, been touched by the numinous. In the battering of daily life, its repetitions, its disappointments, its continuing stresses, such moments are precious. And those moments do deserve to be honored.

What is the *numinous*, you ask? The idea comes from a Latin verb *numen*, which means "to nod or beckon."

Thus, something reaches out to us, and touches us, and summons us. If there were not something in us wanting to be touched, perhaps desperate to be touched, we would remain indifferent. But something within has been called forth, and we remain changed in some way. Rilke's poem, "On the Archaic Torso of Apollo," illustrates this summons. The speaker is examining a weather-beaten, time-worn statue of the god and then realizes that something in the inert yet animated stone is examining him in turn. The poem ends with a seeming non sequitur: "You must change your life." The speaker has been lifted out of the horizontal play of days into some vertical encounter, some encounter with the mysterious other which resonates from without and summons the mysterious other he carries from within himself. Having had this meeting, he cannot return to the old selfhood. He must change his life. So, too, T. S. Eliot's magus in "The Journey of the Magi" had no idea what he experienced in Bethlehem before the infant in the stable, but he now knows that he is no longer home at home, no longer one with these once familiar but now alien people clutching their alien gods.

No wonder these folks have this thought come to them. It did to me, too. I shudder within, nonetheless, for I know what a true tale of tears such a process as analytic training can be. No one goes through it without adding some new scars. No one in those seminars is spared the recrudescence of the old parental material that they thought they left behind decades earlier. No one is spared sibling rivalries with other candidates with all the messiness of family dynamics that seems to follow in our wake. And most difficult of all, no one is spared living for several years in considerable ambiguity. The human ego was not built for ambiguity. It is built for clarity, decisiveness, and as much control as it can wrest from this fractious world. But all three of these, and many more shadow issues, inevitably arise in training institutes in all parts of the world.

Usually, folk's ardor cools when I have them read the requirements of entrance, and the layers of testing that are part of the training process. In the end, it is a personal encounter with one's own soul, and the great unfinished business we drag behind us, more than an academic exercise. (In sum, beware of self-knowledge—you might not like that person you meet.) Some of the quickest to bail are those who come with the greatest of academic talent because all that gets in the way, as you saw in the essay above where what we have become is now our chief obstacle. Some of the most facile minds freeze, wilt, sputter out when confronted by their demons as the process inevitably evokes.

Most central to the training process is one's personal analysis which is meant to include hundreds of hours of intensive self-encounter spread over many years. Added to that is one's repeated meeting with one's review committee, whose job is to observe the process unfolding. I remember a candidate coming in for a first interview who said, based on his prior academic experience, "I understand you are here to help me through the process." "No, we are not," said a colleague quietly. He assumed she had not understood his point, so he repeated it, and she repeated, "No we are not." That, then, led to an interesting conversation.

One can labor for years, pass exams, write papers, be highly credentialed, and still be adjudged unready for promotion to the next stage of the process. That qualitative analysis, flawed and subjective as it may be, is nonetheless a good faith effort to take seriously Jung's admonition to all wounded healers that one cannot take a patient any further than one has traveled oneself. One cannot hold, contain, understand, and perhaps facilitate a process one has not suffered oneself.

When my family and I arrived that first year in Zürich, 1977, it was a few August days after Elvis died. I was surprised to see a rare graffito on the Swiss pristine walls:*Elvis lebt*. Not only did I little understand his universal appeal, but also how little I understood what life continuing after death really meant. We stayed the first week in a pension, a boarding house for transients. All through that first night, after I had schlepped eight suitcases up the stairs to the fourth floor, I could only hear the streetcar below as it hit its brakes for the stop. In the 747 flight across the ocean, and through the night above those tempestuous waves, the Muzak played "Hotel California" over and over. "You can check out any time you like, but you can never leave."I laid in the darkness and thought, "What have I done? I have brought my family for one year on this fool's journey, and now I am in this place and do not even know the next step to take."

The pension quickly ate up our portable cash while I learned that there was a sizeable, and changing, difference between the U.S. dollar and the Swiss franc. But not to worry. I had loans coming from New Jersey where we lived at the time, and they would cover all this. Except they didn't come and didn't come. I waited frantically for those checks to come until December of that year, just as the dollar was plummeting against the Swiss franc. Finally, it arrived, and, for example, a check for $10,000 was now worth about six thousand.... How had that happened? Well, thanks to the parochial sensibility of America, which pays little attention to the rest of the world, the dollar had fallen from rough parity with the franc to about half of what it was when I contracted the loans in New Jersey in June. But what happened to our loan? No, not the international fluctuation of currencies, but how had our checks not arrived? The answer came when I saw the envelope. At that time, the first-class stamp in America was thirteen cents. To send a letter overseas, it took at least a massive twenty-six cents via airmail. Some genius in New Jersey did not know that, pasted a thirteen-cent stamp, and the envelope went surface via ship, wound up in a British dock strike, and finally arrived, having lost nearly 45% of its value. So, that first month was nothing but panic, and looking for work. And, oh yes, we had hired a company to help us find work in Switzerland, only to learn on the ground that the Swiss are fierce in granting work permits and without one of those, you can't work.

In two weeks, we had found a decent apartment, met some nice Swiss, and I began to clean houses for a massive CHF 6/hour, roughly four dollars per hour. For that I cleaned toilets and so on, and when you mean "clean," you don't know clean until you mean Swiss clean. So, I started visiting language schools with the only portable skill I had, the English language. I must have visited more than a dozen until I walked into one that had had an instructor just bail on them hours before. It was Thursday, and the class began Monday. They were desperate too. I took the class, and in six weeks our first evaluations showed my students had done better than the other Swiss instructors. In time, I had three classes and was earning blessed CHF, the only currency that mattered. When I went into class, the students, all mid-life, were sitting ram-rod straight with notebooks to take down the dicta of the Holy Ghost, or something. In time, we learned to have fun. One student had such a revelation when he learned what the word *money* meant. He knew the complete lyrics to the ABBA song "Money, Money, Money" but didn't know what he was singing. We had lots of fun after they learned to relax and experience the joy rather than the burden of learning, and I learned to love them as I have always loved students.

Meanwhile, my wonderful family was adjusting to the rigors of living in a foreign culture. Because those checks had not arrived, we had to put our dear children, Taryn and Tim, in the Swiss school instead of the international school to which they had been admitted. In a few weeks, they were speaking quite passible Swiss German while the adults were still struggling. Later they looked back on this as a great adventure, and it was; and yet I still feel bad for what they had to endure.

About two weeks after we had moved into this apartment, the clouds finally parted, and I saw the Eastern Alps for the first time. I said, in awe, "the gods." That is where the gods lived, and we were this close to them.

When I went to the Jung Institute, then on Gemeinde-strasse 27, it was a dreary massive stone walk-up with tiny consulting rooms and small classrooms. The Sekretariat, the office staff, were Swiss, officious and rather nasty. When I asked for help on housing and employment they said simply, in Darwinian terms, if you are meant to get through here, you will find a way. Later, I came to understand what this inhospitable façade meant: *this is part of your individuation process. You must live it through, or go home.* The head of the library confronted me sternly one day: "Herr Hollis. *Eselsohren, Eselsohren!*" Now, I ask you, what is the right response to that? "Asses ears? Asses ears?" I had committed the cardinal Swiss sin of folding a page to mark a spot and turned it in that way. For a while, I thought I was going to see the *Fremdepolizei,* the foreign police, who kicked more than one student out of the country.

It was a crumbling building, and Zürich at times a dismal place to live, but we made Swiss friends that abide to this day. When my family returned home, and I did repeatedly, it was now with a growing ache for that challenge that our experience provided there. For the next years, I went through the hermetic process of working in America, teaching and learning in Switzerland, and passing back and forth between customs over and over and over. (Stephen Dunn said he always saw only my back departing for somewhere else during those years.) I think I spent more money on *Swissair* than analysis at times. Throughout this, my American teaching income went to support the family, and my Swiss income paid for rent, food, classes, and analysis in Zürich.

All this is the easy part. Zürich winters are mostly grey with rain, and those stunning views of the Alps are rare. I had colleagues back in the U.S. telling me how lucky I was to have the opportunity for skiing in the Alps. I didn't tell them that I was living in a hovel, eating soup and bread only, and running from classes to analysis to teaching and back again. Because I proved to be a good teacher, I was recommended to teach upper-echelon executives at a nearby factory. We, too, started off formally, but in time befriended each other, and this desolate foreigner was invited to their homes, a grace for which I am still so thankful. I taught them more than English. I taught them what it meant to be American, in the best sense of that word. We read an article about the browning of the Black Forest in Germany, and when I said, Switzerland had to convert to lead free gasoline, they said, "But you can't retool a whole country." I pointed out that America had shifted some time earlier, and today when I drive there, all their stations offer only *Bleifrei* petrol. In another key cultural exchange, I learned the execs were anxious because their children were taking the *Matura*, an exam given around age fourteen that determined whether they went into the university, trade schools, or the work force. I told them no one knows what they want to do at fourteen. "But," one retorted, "you can't just go change your life!" I said, "What do you think this forty-year-old is doing in your country?" In America I was a tenured professor with a lifetime job, and here I was teaching English and cleaning houses in their country, some of it "*Schwarzarbeit*, black work," under the table, which could get me kicked out very quickly. Their eyes opened wide as they considered the ramifications. It's possible that they remembered those cultural exchanges more than the new English vocabulary.

Meanwhile, it was so miserable living alone. I recall buying a jar of what I thought was chicken and got home and found I had bought pig knuckles. But it added to my vocabulary. Every day was a classroom, and often the lessons were harsh. Once I received a letter from my dear son Tim who had had hand-copied the front page of the *Philadelphia Inquirer* to send to his dad. I wept, and wept, to know such love, and these decades later, I am flush with gratitude still. Zürich's winter with its months of grey mist and drizzle had only rare reminders that there is a sun. I was so broke there that for my "entertainment" I rode one of the fourteen tramlines in order to get out of the room. At one time, I had memorized the over 150 tram stops in the city. Having a student's monthly pass, or abonnement, I could ride "free" all day, every day. So much for skiing in the Alps. Yes, there were some wealthy widows at the Institute, and occasionally, culture vultures who dropped in and had a good life, but most of us were pretty bedraggled and eking out a living. As my Montreal friend, Jan Bauer, reminded me, our analysts didn't tell us how to get rid of our depressions, but more likely to go back to our flats, and sit with that darkness till we went crazy, went home, or the meaning of the depression revealed itself to us. For most of us—Jan, Guy, Priscilla, Gary, Dennis—far flung across the region and rarely seeing each other, it was the dark night of the soul. They are the survivors. I don't recall the names of those who went home.

So, the six years wore on, shuttling between the U.S. and CH, between family, academia, an internship in a psychiatric hospital, analysis, and coping with the Spartan life abroad. Even at the time it seemed madness, and perhaps was, and yet I could not stop. I knew I was on the track of something necessary and without which my spiritual life was at stake. While I was doing my best to cover everything, I never forgot, nor do I to this day, the family sacrificing at home also. That was a daily crucifixion experience for me.

Decades later, I am still riven by this twin calling to serve others and serve the soul. Jung said so often that such impossible dilemmas must only be endured until their meaning is revealed. (Neurosis, he also said, is suffering that has not yet found its meaning.) As I mentioned in the essay earlier in this book, slowly we all had to unpack our defense systems, live in the terrible in-between of uncertain duration, and perhaps come out the other side of the dark wood. Our Zen-like paradox was what had brought us thus far, and often "successfully," and was now our deepest obstacle. During this difficult time, my wife and I decided to divorce, as amicably as one can ever separate. But for our dear Taryn and Tim, we had been separate in our trajectories for many years. My Midwestern "good guy, never quit, never fail" sense of self was my final, most formidable obstacle. Finally, after many dreams pointing in the same direction, I felt completely defeated. My analyst, who was a socially conservative Swiss, said, "I now believe the divorce should happen. And you should not feel guilty because this is a decision made far deeper than your ego." And so we did, and my wife (now deceased) and I remained friends and co-partners in parenting the children up to her last days on this earth. I went there seeking, in part to "save" the marriage, and learned that it shouldn't be saved, for the persons we were when we contracted the relationship were no longer viable—in fact, they both had died years before. (Despite my analyst's sage advice about guilt, I never yet forgave myself for this "failure," even though I know that is unfinished business on my individuation agenda.) For the next and last two years of training, though single, I did not have a single date, although I had females who were friends. I had no hope for, even desire for, another intimate relationship.

The hinge of history had swung, not as some New Age spiritual ascent, but as a voyage to darkest Hell. (That was what Jung warned as cited above.) No ascent without descent. Doesn't sell many books, but those books that do don't work anyhow. So, one can see how I often shudder when someone says, "I think I will become a Jungian analyst." I never say this, but I always pause and think, "You want to go to Hell, and perhaps not come back? You want to undergo years of analysis, critical scrutiny, papers, exams, and perhaps still be turned down at the end?" But I am Midwestern in origin and always polite. I wasn't able to solve that complex in Zürich either.

I hesitate to include this section in this, my most revealing public disclosure, for it may seem to undermine the tone and tenor of the rest of the essay. But it *is* the rest of the story. When I was reaching the end of my time in Zürich, in fact just three weeks before leaving, an American patient asked if I knew an American working in the Jung Institute library. I said I didn't know there was an American there. I had probably said hello to her in German, assumed she was Swiss because of her appearance and attire, but I decided I would say hello the next time to this mysterious American while I was visiting the library. After all, someone to talk to in English....And so, with days left in my stay in Switzerland, I met Jill. She told me marriage had brought her to Switzerland, and a divorce with two children also had left her to fend for herself. When I departed for America, I told her I was going to come back to see her. She doubted I would return. But I did, for her. Two years after that initial meeting, we married.

The story could end there, but I have to tell the reader one more thing, namely, how one has to sometimes surrender to the absolute mystery of things. My first dream upon arriving for my first hour of analysis six years earlier shook my foundations. I was a knight on the ramparts of a medieval castle which was under siege. The air was thick with arrows, and I felt as if the castle might fall. At the edge of the forest, I could see that a witch was directing the assault. (Was there ever a more archetypal mid-life, middle passage, dream than this?) My analyst said that I had to lower the drawbridge and go out and meet that witch and find out why she was so upset with me. I remember thinking, "Are you nuts? She's trying to kill me!" But in for a penny, in for a pound. Don't come this far and not continue the journey.

Six years later, my last dream in analysis was, get this: I was standing under an arch at the entrance to Graceland—yes, that one, Elvis's estate, which I had never seen in person. From the mansion came this beautiful woman singing this ethereal melody and strewing rose pedals. As she neared me, I thought, "This is no ordinary human; this is a goddess; this is Aphrodite." (Jungians can't help themselves but talk this way.) She reached me, smiled, and gave me a handful of rose petals. The analyst leaned back, remembering where we had started, in the grip of a terrible Anima depression, and said, "You have done your inner work. Now she will come to you in the outer world." A couple of days later, she did. She had been beneath my nose the whole time, working part-time in the *Bibliothek* of the Jung Institute. And we are now nearing our fortieth wedding anniversary. Apparently, some trips to Hades are worth it, a few even have a happy ending.

CHAPTER FIVE

Shipwreck: The Importance of Failure in Our Lives

This essay explores the importance of failure, and the risk of a life too comfortable, protected, or avoidant. Sooner or later, life brings most of us to our knees. How we respond to that, whether we get up and find resources within we did not know existed theretofore, may well determine the whole trajectory of our life beyond that dismal hour.

"The man with the clear head is the man who... looks life in the face, realizes that everything in it is problematic, and feels himself lost. And this is the simple truth—that to live is to feel oneself lost—he who accepts it has already begun to find himself, to be on firm ground. Instinctively, as do the shipwrecked, he will look round for something to which to cling, and that tragic, ruthless glance, absolutely sincere, because it is a question of his salvation, will cause him to bring order into the chaos of his life. These are the only genuine ideas; the ideas of the shipwrecked. All the rest is rhetoric, posturing, farce. He who does not really feel himself lost, is without remission; that is to say he never finds himself, never comes up against his own reality."

Ernest Becker, The Denial of Death.

The human ego is a fragile, porous thing, and generally risk-averse. It is pieced together over the decades from splintered shards of experience. When we are born, we have no ego, no sense of *me* and *not-me*. But out of that miasmic wash of events, increasingly, the split off shards of traumata begin to coalesce, adhere, and the infant slowly realizes that the other is really "other." This split between subject and object is the requisite for consciousness. Such consciousness is inherently painful to the ego, which accounts not only for the continuing appeal of drugs, alcohol, compelling attractions and distractions, and simplistic philosophies of life, but also for the general immaturity that characterizes so much of popular culture.

I have seen a photograph of a baby with its mouth completely over the cheekbone of its mother. Clearly, once contained wholly by her, he longs to consume her and reenter that primal syzygy, that oceanic fusion with the other. So powerful is this drive that it shows up in all of our subsequent relationships in some form or another. Its archaic power creates what some years ago I called *The Eden Project*, a study of the psychodynamics of relationship. The Eden Project metaphor allusively intimates the desire to re-connect to the source, even be subsumed by that primal other. (Adam and Eve could eat of the Tree of Experience, that is nature naturing, but they become conscious of separation, estrangement, when they eat of the Tree of Knowledge. From that moment on, they are serving split agendas—the claim of instinct and the diverging claim of their social environment.) When this archaic, regressive agenda triumphs over the maturation process, as it so often does, the relationship is regressive, infantilized, and in service to the annihilation of consciousness. The continuing appeal of "romance" serves this archaic hope that one can fuse with the other and be transported once more to the time before consciousness. What do you think the phrase *le petit morte*, French for "the little death," or orgasm means, other than the temporary annihilation of consciousness arising from fusion with the other?

In that book, *The Eden Project: In Search of the Magical Other*, I suggest that in every relationship there is an ongoing tension between this archaic phantasy that hopes the partner will prove to be the "good" parent, versus the summons to the difference-driven dialectic which alone brings about growth and maturation. It is not an accident that our ancestors worked so hard to create rites of passage for they knew how strong this regressive surge within was for each person.

Please recall that in *Symbols of Transformation*, published in 1912, Jung noted that each morning there is a part of us that wakens, and immediately desires to drown it its own source, to fall back into the sleep of childhood and avoid the terrifying demands of daily conflict and struggle. That tendency, he notes, was opposed by those great psychotherapeutic systems known as the tribal mythologies and rites whose purpose was to steer libido in the direction of adulthood, lest the tribe be left with only children at the helm of the ship of state. But what happens when the rites, the affect-laden images that mobilize libido, disappear? What happens when youth has no real separations going on, no immersion in the supports and challenges of adult life, no wise mentors to help them bridge from childhood into proto-adulthood? What happens when they have video games rather than tests of their mettle, when they have porn instead of the real demands of real relationship, when they have no wise elders to share the secrets of the tribe with them? (This is not only a Western development.

Young women in Japan [20-30] are presently complaining that their male counterparts no longer are even interested in having sex with them. And *The Washington Post* reported that many, many young Chinese are resisting entering the workforce, using a phrase that translates as "lying flat," that is, avoiding work wherever possible. Then, similarly, we recall the essentially adolescent American culture with all its distractions, hubbubs, and soporifics in which we currently swim.)

Currently, I have several clients whose post-college children are still living at home, still expecting some great job to land in their laps, and still assuming that all the electronic gear they have teethed upon are guaranteed in the Constitution. One young college graduate recently said, after his parents implored him to find work, that he wouldn't dream of taking a job until he was offered a six-figure inducement out of his comfy life at home. (!) Most of them assume that a middle or upper-middle class existence is their right rather than understanding that someone before them had to work very, very hard to earn it. My father was pulled out of eighth grade, (eighth grade!) and sent to work the rest of his life. My mother learned to type and sew. Both of them knew early that they were bound to rise each morning and go to work to keep the wolf from the door. When I saw them, I knew I was to do likewise, and am still doing it. The only difference is, because of my privilege of getting the education denied to them, I was able to merge work with vocation and to love the amalgamas I still do. Indeed, at 81, I haven't retired because I still haven't found a better way to spend my life than what I am presently privileged to do. They didn't have the choices I gained, and I am daily grateful for their sacrifices that allowed me to live a larger journey. (Of course, herein I am describing First World Problems, and with even that, only a segment of our people. Many today struggle to survive, every day, in often demeaning ways.)

But what is the purpose of rehearsing these obvious points? Much has been written about our immature culture—a culture that wants what it wants when it wants it, is sometimes more afraid of a needle prick than gasping their Covid-ridden lungs out in a hospital, that believes that materialism, hedonism, narcissism, distraction are the way to spend this brief journey. What possible role might risk, adversity, *failure* play in this new phantasy world?

The bottom line is that we grow most from hardship, adversity, failure. How can any of us grow without risk, without getting knocked down, and then getting right back up and forging ahead? But before visiting what rises to meet us in our various shipwrecks, let us briefly revisit the wisdom of our ancestors.

Our distant ancestors contrived rites of passage to help youth, especially boys, but girls too, in different ways, into the mystery of adulthood. Yes, they were simpler societies where life was, in the words of Thomas Hobbes, "poor, nasty, brutish, and short" and puberty was the mid-life crisis for many. There was no central headquarters for these elaborate rituals, no common tom-toms sending out guidelines, but so many of these quite remote societies nonetheless practiced them precisely because they, too, perceived the inordinate desire of our psyche to be left to creature comforts, to avoid conflict, labor, and hardship. If they had given into those tendencies, there would be no adults on the scene to tend to the necessary tasks of survival.

While the local rituals varied immensely, in particular, the general form, shape, and progressive stages of the passages were strikingly similar.

The first stage was *Departure*. The child wasn't given a choice, no engraved invitation; often he was "kidnapped" in the middle of the night by elders with painted faces or masks representing not relatives down the row, but visitants from the spirit world, even the gods themselves in their holy epiphanic visitation. The second stage was *Death*. Some ceremony of death was enacted whereby the child and his psychology of dependence was slain forever. No going back. The third stage was the *Ordeal* wherein the youth was subjected to hardship, survival, endurance, and often ritual wounding. This last we might consider child abuse but was symbolic of the necessary *quid pro quo* of life: to get something, you also have to sacrifice something. The next stage, and sometimes these last two were reversed, was the *Teaching*. The elders passed on the tribal secrets at three levels. The "archetypal," tribal frame conveyed who the gods were, along with their tribal foundation stories of origin and purpose. The second layer conveyed the civil polity: the rights, duties, expectations of adults in that culture. The third was occupational—how our people survive through hunting, gathering, warfare, agriculture, and so on. Today we give kids some computer skills and say "go get a job somewhere." The last stage was the *Return* to the conventional world, but only after the ordeal in which the youth had learned to deal with fear, to find resources around, and to find resilience within. Yes, it was a simpler society, but they did produce something nearer adulthood than we tend to achieve. All of us would consider the treatment above harsh, but their world was harsh, and survival no sure thing. Without adults no society can survive. Do we have adults, many of them? Having big bodies, big bank accounts, and big roles to play in life does not an adult make, as we see all around us.

Dr. Nan Henderson, founder of the institute *Resiliency in Action,* is one contemporary who grasps the necessity of challenge, of completing tasks, and of facing one's fears. Having achieved success working with adolescents, she has found that something within them actually wants challenge, wants to be tested, even in the presence of all the distractions, drugs, and inducements to psychic slumber that our contemporary culture makes available. Every time I pass an athletic field I want to be out there once again in the rough and tumble of the scrimmage, even get roughed up a bit, and to find what next I am called to do, and what resources I will need to bring to the challenge. When I wrote my old college football coach in preparing the book on men mentioned above, he wrote back his wisdom these many, many years later: "You get knocked down, Jimmy, and you get up, fasten your chin-strap, and get ready for the next play." I cannot tell the reader how important that was to me when I was young, and how much it has helped through the decades since.

While most would agree the first duty of a parent is to protect the child we are given, we learn fairly soon how impossible that project truly is. For those of you who are parents, or grand-parents, you know well the mix of joy and worry those children brought you. Yes, it is demonstrably clear that when we are given that bundle of joy, the willfully obscure gods who just gifted us send along a lifetime of worry also. Many moons ago I confessed in the chapter on "Anxiety," in the 1996 book *Swamplands of the Soul*, that, accompanying the joy at the birth of my first grandchild Rachel Erin, was the thought "Here is someone else to worry about." Admitting even then that such a thought at such an hour may be neurotic, it is also realistic, especially if magnified by my childhood home where anxiety and worry were the stuff of daily life—as palpable and as present as the Cheerios at the breakfast table. So, it is natural to worry about our children. Something terrible *will* happen to them, sooner or later. And we *will* lose them, or they us, sooner or later.

Well, now, having lifted your spirits immensely, what are we to make of this dilemma? I can truly say that all my years of worry did not keep my son from dying before me, or my younger brother. And yet, it seems it is the urgent province of the sensitive parent to worry, and to be as protective as possible. I recall reading a poem many years ago which I have not been able to find again. In it, a new father is hovering over the crib of his child and imagining all the terrible things that might happen to her in the forlorn hope that if he can touch all the bases, such dreadful event would not, according to his magical thinking, happen. And yet, he was terrified that he was probably not remembering all of those dire possibilities. "I am up at midnight, writing this," was his last line, as best I can recall. I know that brother's feelings well.

In my childhood home, fraught as it was with an omnipresent worry of all kinds, I grew up with the natural desire of any child for some adventure, some exploration of the world. When I saw that my gestures in that direction triggered waves of anxiety in the home, rising like platoons of gnats from the unclean stalls of history, I learned not to ask, and often to go underground. So, I walked to neighbors' homes, climbed trees with friends, sometimes roofs, and imagined we could see the whole world from that vantage. Little did I know I was preparing for over a million air miles of flight later, looking down on the ant-like forms below. It's not that we were being derelict; we were exploring the world. That is what we are here to do—what children need to do. My parents' fears were natural, and their protective measures understandable. Had they been successful, and they nearly were, they would have broken my spirit.

My maximum life height was 5' 8", which in the world of sports is small. As a small guy, I was naturally afraid of being beat up by big guys. So what's a small guy to do with that fear? Play football of course. My parents naturally forbade me from going out for football, but by the time I was a junior, I slipped away from them, practiced, and somehow made the team. By then, it was a de facto misdemeanor. It would be more problematic for them to take me away from the game than to let me continue. I rewarded their faith in me and fear of the world by breaking my thumb, which of course validated their theories. In college, I played and lettered for a Division III team. Now, Division III is not serious football but to us it was, and two of my teammates, an end and a linebacker, were invited to the training camps of the then-named Baltimore Colts, and the Dallas Texans. Neither proved fast enough for the pros, but it demonstrated that we did play football of some kind.

Now, why did I do such a foolish thing as play football when it was clearly meant for bigger guys? The answer is simple, I was more afraid of my fear than I was of them, and I was more afraid of being afraid to not risk it. That is the gist of it. I don't expect the reader to understand, and I imagine some astute reader will use my own (adult) words against me and repeat my oft-cited question: "What does fear make you do, or keep you from doing?" All I can say is, this is the adult me speaking, and I am glad the younger me was more afraid of fear than getting beat up by big guys. It was some preparation for what was to come.

When our ancient ancestors devised the elaborate rites of passage with their multi-stages of trial, they always included some form of ritual wounding—incision, circumcision, a severed ear lobe, and so on. While today we would consider such practices barbaric, and child endangerment, they understood the deep message each of us has to internalize:"Life is for real; it's going to hurt you, and you have to bear it and go through it. Moreover, if you want to step into the larger enterprise of the adult, there is a *quid pro quo*. You can't remain a whiny baby all your life. If you want something: go earn it, pay for it, and then you deserve it."

In all the years since, given my working-class family of origin, I never expected anything from others that I hadn't personally earned. How many later times in life, whether in times of immense physical trial, heart-bending grief, or the descent into the dark valley of aging and infirmity have I drawn on that experience and pushed through the temptations of despair or capitulation. How removed all this is from our natural parental desire to protect our children from hardship. In no way do I support pushing a child to do something he or she does not really wish, but there will be times when that child has to face itself, its fear, its dependency, risk something important to them, and push through it to the other side.

In the book on men, *Under Saturn's Shadow: The Wounding and Healing of Men*, I mentioned an incident worth repeating here. It was Labor Day morning in New Jersey. The cool air of the ocean was rolling onshore and met the departing warmth of summer's blast, and formed a mist which shrouded the landscape. As we rose to take our mighty Lhasa Apso "Shadrach" for his morning oblations, we could hear the cadence of the high school team across the street as they did their calisthenics. My wife, with a kindly maternal instinct, proffered the suggestion that the coaches should have let those teens sleep-in for the holiday. I replied with a series of observations, each more opaque than its predecessor. No, I said, in so many words, "They want to be out there, not sleeping in bed. They are looking for their brothers out there. They are also looking for their fathers out there, those who will teach, mentor them, give them a glimpse of adulthood. And...and they are looking to get hurt out there, knowing intuitively that it will be the first of many hurts, and knowing that they need to start dealing with it now." These comments were no doubt peculiar to my partner, especially the last. I didn't go on to tell her that I was pleased when I broke that thumb. It gave me a chance to go through something. I was not suggesting that those ideas were consciously present to those sweating young men, but I do know that it was in their unconscious, and that these deeply driving motives were powerful enough to get them out of bed early and into the cadence.

In telling my dear partner that those youth wanted to forsake the comforts of a holiday sleep-in, I knew they were wanting to test themselves, to feel that communal energy of kinship libido that the team provides. They were desperate to find wise counselors who could help them deal with fear and perform even while afraid. And they also knew they needed to be tested, to be hurt, banged up, in order to deal with the child inside and see if their emerging adult might show up instead. Intuitively, they knew they needed to be challenged, pummeled, and knocked to the ground just to see if they would get up again. If they could, if they did, they would know so much more about their lives and their possibilities, and they would know they had something within that would carry them through. Unconsciously, this was part of their rehearsal for becoming a functioning adult. Pity anyone who does not know that for he or she will live in floating dread of the uncertainties of the coming hours.

By no means am I suggesting that sports are for everyone. Not at all. Nor am I really suggesting that your child should try out for football, soccer, lacrosse, or some other contact sport. (Neither of my own children were interested in contact sports, but they had to find their way through other venues.) I am suggesting that we all have to face what such moments of hardship, defeat, dismay bring to us—even shipwreck. We may not play football, but sooner or later we will find dark hours in which our souls are up for grabs. We will experience physical and emotional pain, enough to break the will, and then....then, what will we do? Those who had the experience of those hours of wreckage will draw upon it many times later. And those who did not, will often ache for not knowing what they could draw upon in their difficult hours. Those who did not, have other appointments to keep, sooner or later, for what rites today help us face our fears, grow up, and push through to be present in the fullest way we can manage?

All of us have appointments with shipwreck, despite debilitating hours of fear and impotence. Each day is a summons to get on the field of play as it shows up in our diverse lives, even as each day it proves so easy to slip-slide away into avoidances. How many times in rehab for surgeries I imagined myself back on that field, and summoned an old discipline to further the task of healing. For all the failures and avoidances of my life, how many times today do I still pass a football field, see the youth out there, and would trade it all just to be lining up with them. *Huddle up, call the play, run it, get knocked down, tighten the helmet strap, huddle up, and get set for the next one. It's fourth quarter, third and long. You're in the game. The next play is coming, now.* All this is but an old man's foolishness, of course; but then if you ever really heard that cadence, it is magical, and one never forgets it—it resonates in the heart's systole and diastole like the rhythm of life and death.

All of us, in varying degrees, are riven with self-doubt, insecurity, debilitating complexes, all of us—myself included, to this very day. It never goes away. The question, then, is do we show up and meet the demands of life when they come or remain mewling children looking for some parental figure to fix it all for them? We all need to find out what we can do, how high we can fly, what the limits of our talents and capacities are, and then make the most of it. All of us have to try to separate from the infantilizing and seductive culture all around us that distracts, diverts, and denies our summons to personhood. Fear is ubiquitous; only the psychotic or the stoned are fearless. The question is, what do you do when you are afraid? Do you keep avoiding, slip-sliding away, or show up as best you can? Most of the world, both afraid and at the edge of perishing from want, war, or worry, don't have the luxury of our distractions. Every day is sheer struggle for survival. But do the rest of us, privileged whether we want to admit that or not, show up as ourselves? The pragmatic questions always are *what does fear, self-doubt make you do or keep you from doing with your life*?

When this journey ends, if we are conscious, can we say that with all the screw-ups, defeats, and losses we did our best? Can we say that when adversity came to us, as it always will, we learned that there was in us a resilience we did not know was there? Can we realize that nature has provided us, as with our ancestors, the inherent strength to see all things through? Can we know life will not spare us hardship but that we can also find resources we did not know we had? I have no truck with the fatuous statement that "God gives people no test they cannot withstand." I have seen, and sometimes worked with, broken souls, shattered spirits. And yet, with all that, after all that, I have often seen that out of hardship, adversity, and failure, many may still rise from the ashes and find some part of their life and their individuation intact and healthy.

Some readers will know that I spent all of last year dealing with prostate and bladder cancer, and remain in watchful treatment, plus book-ended by both total knee and hip replacements. I swore from the beginning that my mantra would be "militant submission;" that is to say, I submitted to mortality, and the disorders of the flesh, as we all must, and yet chose not to allocate more of my psychic economy than those treatments demanded. During that time, rising often at 5:15 a.m. for 40 radiation treatments, I continued my practice, taught via Zoom, and got two books out. This example is *not* self-congratulatory. Quite the contrary, this process was quite selfish—I chose to maintain my engaged life as best I could, transferring only the energy needed for treatments, and kept the rest to use for the life I still find meaningful. During that whole time, I was often annoyed, but never depressed. I knew that whatever the treatments, and the follow-ups for years to come, personal dignity and spiritual independence are never lost unless we give them away.

Sometimes we need to know when life is too ordered for us to know the outer edge of what is enough. As the mad visionary William Blake wrote, "The road to Excess leads to the Palace of Wisdom." How would we know that without pushing the envelope somewhere, sometime? Each of us needs to experience risk and shipwreck sometimes because out of that we have an invitation to figure out who we really are, and what matters to each of us. In his poem "Odysseus's Secret," Stephen Dunn writes of that ancient mariner, and all of us, "A man finds his shipwrecks." There is a shipwreck unique to us, *our* shipwreck, and it is waiting for us to show up. What we do after the shipwreck is what ultimately defines our life.

There are many who skate through life unperturbed, some with luck, some with naiveté, and some with sheer opacity of soul. None of this shipwreck talk will make any sense to any of them. But there are those out there who picked themselves up off the floor, those who emerged from the crash, those who listened when something inside demanded they persist, and from then forward they knew that something supports them from within when the outer world has fallen apart. To know what supports us when nothing supports us is a genuine treasure. As the Persian poet Hafiz put it in "A Divine Invitation," "We can come to God / dressed for dancing / or / Be carried on a stretcher / to God's ward." Either way, life will ask us to show up, sooner or later.

So those helicopter parents are not helping their children, even the ones buying their kids into colleges. What will their child do later when life comes knocking at the door? What will they do when the dark gods show up in the dark hours? What will any of us do until we find out the hard way? What resources will we find when our ship wrecks? We may find that we are more buoyant than we thought; we may find that we rise back to the surface and swim on toward the beckoning shore.

CHAPTER SIX

Doing Difficult Therapy

Therapy derives from the Greek therapeuein, *which means "to attend, or listen to," and* psyche *is the Greek word for "soul." So, psychotherapy is about attending to or listening to the soul. Already, we are in some different territory than most folks imagine. The moment we invoke "soul," we raise the question of meaning. Three groups of people require especially complex approaches to this matter of attending soul: couples, men, and those with spiritual immaturity. Why difficulties are inherent to each of those groups and how one might begin addressing such challenges is our subject. If the reader is not a therapist, no matter; the issues raised herein touch all of us in very subtle but telling ways.*

I. With Couples

After perhaps twenty years of doing therapy with couples, I stopped and shifted exclusively to mid- and second-half of life adults. Why is part of the story.

Many times when a couple entered the office and said they wanted to "work on the relationship," it was already too late. Too many pints of blood had drained from the corpus of intimacy for it to be revived. And sustaining it as some sort of bloodless Golem seemed an uninviting prospect. Most often the couples themselves thought of the process as something not unlike a wrestling match wherein the therapist would indicate a point here, a point there, and in the end the therapist would hold up the hand of one of them and declare that person the winner. Naturally, they assumed that their case, their *apologia*, was most worthy of such a prize. Frequently, one of them would expect to be "ambushed" by the deadly cabal of the therapist and their partner. Usually, but not always, this was the man. Therapy already seemed like some sort of "female" thing, and the wife was already miles ahead in marshalling her argumentative points (more about this later in part II).

A few phenomena were noticeable quite early in my experience as a couple's therapist. One was that things said, over and over, at home were sometimes "heard," in a new way, or perhaps even for the first time when it was spoken before a third party, a witness in the court of conjugal litigation. That was useful for it meant that core issues might finally receive the recognition they deserved. Secondly, I found that often one of the pair was far more ready for a deepened conversation than the other. That person often was the woman, though not always (more about this later in part II). So, it was best if each person could also be in therapy with their own counselor, but few folks could manage that financially, and most thought it too demanding emotionally. Naturally, I made what I considered heroic efforts to be a fair, impartial listener. I wanted each to leave, each hour, thinking they had been heard and valued. That is more difficult than it seems. Sometimes I found myself instinctually liking one client more than the other, trusting their accounts more, but my ethical summons was to maintain as much impartiality as possible.

In one memorable example, I worked with a couple whose issues didn't seem to run deep at the time, and the prognosis was favorable. At the end of that calendar year to which each had committed, the husband told me that all the while he was involved with another person, that he had no intention of sustaining the marriage, and that he had planned to leave his wife in my "capable hands" with the assurance that she would have someone to take care of her and clean up the aftermath of the shock. I felt completely betrayed as he had lied to my face over and over for fifty weeks or so, and yet I could do nothing about it. Shortly thereafter, his wife came to me only a few times. I think she always associated me with that dishonest year together, and somehow felt our work irretrievably contaminated. And perhaps it was.

It is the general assumption of the public that the therapist's job is to "save" the marriage, even at all costs. Such advocates do not ask a simple question: Does the soul of each party thrive, grow in this relationship, or is it possible for them to evolve to that place? Yet, for many, the relationship must be saved even if its chief levers are guilting, coercion, sentimentality, and the intimidating weight of collective expectations. I witnessed many thoughtful souls who were more in love with their idea of marriage than the person to whom they were married. How many persons told me, "I knew the day we married I did not want to marry, but....the invitations were all sent out; the relatives had all arrived; my parents would have been devastated; I didn't want to hurt my spouse to be...,"and so on. Choose your reason.

One of the most troubling of human phenomena is that no matter how rotten the outcome, or how compromised the motives, there is always a "good" reason for doing whatever we do. I guess no one sets out to intentionally do something for bad reasons....though we all do, and frequently. As Friedrich Nietzsche said of nations, "It's amazing how good bad reasons and bad music are when one is marching against the enemy." When I was director of the Jung Center of Houston some years ago, an enthusiastic member told me that her close friend, the wife of a national politician, categorically would not come to the Center with its rich offering of speakers and courses. When asked why not, she said, "Because our son saw a Jungian *and* got a divorce. Maybe that Jungian, not me, did a good job in helping the couple with discernment, but to this matriarch, the job of the therapist was to keep them together at any cost. The Jung Center then was just collateral damage."

Sometimes the therapist realizes that the premises which brought the couple together in the first place those years ago was long outlived, or was very troubled in the first place, and that to perpetuate the toxicity now evident would be most regrettable. Of course, merely the presence of suspect founding premises does not mean that the couple might not also evolve toward more mature, more life-giving premises to stay afloat in a new way. But then, their first marriage had to die if the reconstituted second was to have a chance. Some of the happiest moments for me as a couple's therapist occurred on these rather uncommon occasions. And, paradoxically, some of the best work I ever did was facilitate a discernment process in the couple that led to their amicable dissolution. That was not a defeat; it was a successful therapeutic outcome wherein the real question was: does this relationship support the soul of each party, contribute to their growth and independence, or can it be re-engineered so that it might? When the answer is negative, that is always something profound to grieve. Every marriage is an investment in hope, in body, and in soul. When a ship goes down off shore, we may not be able to save the persons on board, but we can grieve their loss, and honor the hopes they had.

Most onerous was the constant tension of juggling sometimes competing interests within the couple themselves. Sometimes one would get up and pace about the room and storm out, but most of the time most folks behaved because they wanted to present their best front to this stranger (a.k.a. the referee) whom they were visiting. Sometimes, a soupcon of violence was present, and more than once I wondered if an aggrieved spouse might decide to shoot the messenger since they didn't like the message the therapy was evoking. I recall one cantankerous physician who alleged in his divorce filings that his wife was having an affair with the therapist because she called me by my first name rather than "Doctor" as the learned doctor insisted in his world. On another occasion when I was directly threatened, I dreamt that I was in some sort of large underground processing center, almost like immigration facilities. I was being interviewed by a government employee and asked where I would like to live. I realized then that I was being inducted into the Witness Protection Program to save my life. In the dream, I thought long and hard about this choice and answered that I declined this offer of protection, that I am a therapist, and that this dreck is what therapists must face in their work. The dream was truly comforting to me for years to come. I was impressed that my psyche could both accurately discern the danger, and yet rise above it and find the larger meaning in my personal fight/flight conflict.

Over many years of doing couples work, I found myself far preferring working one-on-one with someone, and going as deeply into their self-exploration as they could. While I often look back on working with couples, I haven't missed it. I know that any couple is made up of two individuals, and that no relationship with another is going to be more evolved than what each person brings to the table. In *The*

Eden Project: In Search of the Magical Other, I explored how each of us carries archaic images of the "other" in our psyches. On the one hand, we have an intra-psychic imago of the Magical Other who will fix our lives, be the long-sought perfect parent, meet our needs, and if we are really lucky, spare us the burden of growing up. And on the other hand, one often seeks to replicate the vagaries of fate in the choice of a partner, to repeat the abuse, the codependence, the fractious assignment that once came along with living with severely wounded parents. It is the therapist's maieutic task to help clients bring these intra-psychic imagoes to the surface, examine them, and begin the work of outgrowing their regressive matrices and infernal agendas. When one can look within and see all this hidden material, one has a shot at lifting it off of the partner. That is how one moves from romance, seductive as it is, to actually loving the partner. Whatever we of ourselves can lift off our partner is an act of loving them. This work is never-ending because we have so much psychic debris and bilge down in the hold of the ship we sail.

Were I to undertake couples therapy again today, I would promote a greatly modified idea of how to go about it, and I have shared these thoughts with other therapists in seminars and conferences. In *The Eden Project*, I make a few basic but pertinent points about our lives. We are born into radical, traumatic estrangement from the Other through that convulsive event called birth. Naked, defenseless, powerless—why would we not want to crawl back into a safe place? This deep, deep motive, this archaic hope remains with us no matter how big our bodies grow, or our psyches enlarge. It is present, to some degree, in all human relationships. Mature folks can keep it at bay even if they do not know what they are containing. Immature folks, and any of us under considerable stress, cannot. We expect the other to take care of it for us. As understandable as this may be, it is not realistic, not loving the objective otherness of the Other, and just not going to happen. When it does, it infantilizes the relationship, burdens the other, and so often remains the source of sorrow, anger, and contention.

In *The Eden Project,* I identify and propose the "heroic" question:*"What am I asking of the other that I need to be doing for myself?"* I call this "heroic" because it means I lift it off of my partner and take it on myself. In that moment, the relationship moves from the phantasy of romance to the act of really risking loving the other. What I do not burden my partner with is one less thing for them to carry. It is mine, and in our heart of hearts, we all, all, know that. Growing up means we have to accept that responsibility. If we don't, the relationship will remain forever disappointing and burdensome to both parties.

Today, I would ask something like the following questions more directly. I know I asked them in some form in those old days, but never as clearly and as systematized as here. As each of these questions has enormous heuristic value, and may open up a lot of material for digestion, this question protocol may need to transpire over several sessions.

1. Ask each party in the relationship to pull back, reflect awhile, and then *convey their private and deepest fears.* What wakes them at night at the hour of the wolf? What has likely been a life-long fear and shows up in many protean forms? This is not a question about the partner, or even the relationship, but about their own voyage through this large, scary passage we call life. It may strike the reader that this is a peculiar question to ask. But I beg indulgence on one matter:

my experience has told me that more of our behaviors, avoidances, stuck places arise out of fear, and fear management, than any other causal factor. When the therapist can get the party to focus on their life-long fears, the spouse usually sits back and looks on in silence, sometimes with respect, sometimes even with wonder. In that narrow moment, they are present to the humanity of their partner, not the categorical projection they have upon the partner. It begins to soften the rancor, perhaps open the heart a bit.

2. Ask each person *what he or she brings to the table which they know is annoying and painful to the other*, that which has so often provoked discord, conflict, hurt. This interrogative shift of focus certainly upsets the "therapist as referee" paradigm. It usually puts folks back on their heels, and one may have to ask it again to make sure to them that we mean it, and that they are to reflect on it for real. If they resist, I would push.

3. Next, ask them to *identify what they might do to lift some burden* off *of their partner*, especially in light of the fact that they have just seen their partner hurting and vulnerable. This question obviously shifts the expected blaming back to each party to ask accountability for what they might concretely do to help the struggling person they see before them.

4. Then ask each person *what their own deepest needs are, and how they are going to try to address them rather than their partner*. This question does not go down well, if any of them do, because of the archaic Edenic phantasy that the other is going to take care of our grocery list of needs. And since they haven't gotten very far with that list, the other is perceived

as a huge failure. This question continues the slow, often agonizing march toward adulthood. Without maturation, the relationship will be stuck at the lowest level of the psychological maturity of one or both of the partners.

5. Then ask them *how they might begin being more aware of the deepest needs of their partner*, and if not wholly supply that need, at least be aware of its presence. Here we approach the fact that in a healthy relationship with another for whom we care, we are both aware of their wounds, their history, and their needs. When possible, we can work with that, and be part of the solution instead of part of the problem. This notion does not obviate or contradict what is written before; it is an acknowledgement of the genuine summons of relationships to help the other, and to care for their well-being.

6. We then ask each person *what baggage they think they have brought into the relationship*—both positive and negative—that now is present in the contemporary hour. The matrix of family life is present to each of us all our lives as the primal model, message, and motive which infiltrates the current dynamics. We either serve those messages, and repeat them, which is by far most common, or we run from them and are caught in over-compensation; or we are trying to "fix" history's format in some forlorn and futile way. We are never wholly free of the old psychological home, the old dynamics. But we don't have to suffer them in perpetuity. Consciousness from time to time can help any of us choose differently, and find a different, better life.

7. Lastly, we ask them, separately and together, *what aspects of the implicit "contract" that brought them*

together have not actually served them. And then we ask their constructive ideas on *what kind of new contract might be "written,"* based on what they now know of each other, and of themselves. This last question opens the real possibility of a new marriage. If the old one was working so well, why have we been in this process? For any to have genuine good will and enthusiasm about a possible alternative future, they have to believe it possible, realistic, and worthwhile. I believe all of these questions can serve that possibility.

If I were starting over today, I would probably assign these questions for each to write out, spend time addressing, and perhaps query each other at home. I cannot guarantee these questions will work, but I think they might. Couples therapy is always attempting or facilitating a conversation which is not happening at home. It is an artificial construct; its intensity risks the whole ballgame; and it asks an awful lot of folks, but it is better than seeing that ship go down with all those good souls on board without an heroic effort to bring them home.

II. *Doing Therapy with Those Strange Creatures Called Men*

I am still surprised, chagrinned, and dismayed at how long it took me to tumble to men's issues. After all, many colleagues, following the courageous example of the feminists, were starting to speak on those issues, and I of course had been living them for half a century when the Jung Society of Philadelphia asked me to speak on the subject in preparation for my old Zürich colleague Guy Corneau's visit and presentation on "Absent Fathers, Lost Sons." Uncharacteristically, I delayed preparing my talk, postponed, procrastinated until time was running out. I finally had to play that old therapist's dirty trick on myself: "What would you say to a client who came to you with this problem?" I knew already: resistance is in direct proportion to fear. So, the topic must be triggering some fears. But what? And a voice from within said, *"But we don't talk about these matters."* Whoo...what was that, where did that come from, and what did it mean?

Suddenly, I knew...as a man I had bred into, conditioned and controlled by the secrets men carry. What secrets? Well, it's not a secret if you tell, is it? But then I knew I had to tell, to spill the beans, and I organized my talk around the secrets, which then poured out of me once I opened the door. When I printed them in *Under Saturn's Shadow: The Wounding and Healing of Men*, I got a lot of responses from men. All of them said thanks because up to that time they always thought that what they felt and believed marked them as failures, poor facsimiles of men, or just insufficient. And then, to my surprise, I got a lot of positive feedback from women who said that the discussion had helped them to know better, and even sympathize, with those strange, often self-destructive, and frequently hidden creatures they call men.

In later years, I was asked by various women's groups to talk to them about those peculiar creatures with whom many of them lived. I appreciated their invitations as not many men's groups would have requested the topic: *how can we understand women better*? I usually began by articulating three propositions, and asked them to imagine they were the defining frames of their lives.

1. Imagine that all of your close friends, here and elsewhere, are cut away from your life forever. Those friends with whom you share your worries about your children, your marriages, your sex life or lack thereof, your body, your troubles in general—they are never again to be available to you.

2. Imagine that your linkage to what you consider your internal guidance system—call it your instinct, or your intuition, or whatever—is severed forever.

3. Imagine that your worth as a human being would forever be measured by your competitive wins or losses, and your general worth contingent on meeting elusive standards of productivity as defined by total strangers.

If they could so imagine, then they would be closer to knowing the daily experience of men: the isolation, the estrangement from self and others, the shame, the rage, and the despair that often expresses itself through acting-out behaviors. Most often those women were appalled, correctly guessing the enormous isolation and self-estrangement such conditions would impose. Many asked "What can we do to help?" Nothing, I said, other than from time to time understand he is crazy for some good reasons, and even he doesn't know why. It's not as personal to you as it may so often seem. Besides that, men have to figure this out for themselves.

Before getting at the meat of this essay, an approach to therapy with men, let me summarize those eight secrets of most men's lives. (There is a much fuller explanation of each of these "secrets" in *Under Saturn's Shadow*, but I give this condensed version to lead into our different focus here.)

1. *Men's lives are as much governed by restrictive role expectations as are the lives of women.*

Women have heroically, and persistently, challenged the role expectations of gender. Men have been slower on the uptake. They have been so deeply conditioned for millennia that to question the contemporary premises of "manhood" is already to risk one's manhood. This attitude will mean that men will fall further and further behind women's liberation toward personhood, which is what is presently happening in virtually every area of their engagement. Because the roles are changing, most men today are between definitions, between roadmaps, and are generally confused and driven to psychological entropy and malaise.

2. *Men's lives are essentially governed by fear.*

Through the millennia, men's chief task was to hide, deny, divert their core fears in the mistaken belief that every other little boy out there was not intimidated by overwhelming challenges and abiding fears of personal inadequacy. This inherent contradiction in men's acculturation means that they are forever invested in pretending, and lying, even lying to themselves. Courage is not the absence of fear, but acting as life demands in the face of it. Recently, in a podcast, the interviewer asked what person in history would I most like to converse with. My first thought was Lincoln, and then I said, "I would like to meet myself as a ten-year-old. I would tell that ten-year-old that he was going to have a much richer life than he could imagine, that his fears were normal and natural, that all the others have the same fears, and tell him to relax a bit and enjoy the world." I know that such advice would have made his life so much better, and mine as well.

3. *The power of the feminine is immense in the psychic economy of men.*

Men are born of women, and most of their early relationships are with women. Yet, their destiny is elsewhere. How can they become a man, whatever that means, with such a paucity of modeling, teaching, and mentoring by their kind? This educational discrepancy is especially deepened since men moved from the land and the crafts to offices and factories and came home dispirited, angry, and often self-medicated.

4. *Men collude in a conspiracy of silence whose aim is to suppress their emotional truth.*

By the time a boy is five or six, he has learned that to express his feelings, cry, or show what is going on inside is risky indeed. He has learned shame, ridicule, bullying, and isolation. If he doesn't want to spend his life in those dismal neighborhoods, he has to keep his mouth shut. In time, keeping his mouth shut so strongly means keeping his mind shut also, and he often loses contact with what he really feels about anything. So, whenever he says, "I don't know—I really don't care what we do," he usually means it because he has lost his inner compass. For many, the chest is an arid zone.

5. *Because men must leave Mother, and transcend the mother complex, wounding is necessary.*

The mother "complex" is not synonymous with the personal mother, though she may play a large role in influencing, programming it. Her needs, her interactions, her enlistment of him in her agendas will substantially alter the course of his life. At the same time, the regressive aspects of his life will show up in his great desire for her to take care of him, to spare him the rigors of the journey ahead. In later life he will have a tendency to burden his partner with a profound ambivalence of both need and fear of encroachment. Our ancestors from all cultures generated rites of passage necessary to mobilize that libido into the psychology and behaviors of manhood. In addition to teaching three spheres of value—the tribal gods and primal stories, the duties and expectations of adulthood, and the practical tasks of daily life—they understood that some form of wounding was necessary to communicate the *quid pro quo* of life. If you want something, you have to pay for it with your labor, your commitment, sometimes your suffering. Truly important things transform that suffering into meaning.

6. *Men's lives are violent because their souls have been violated.*

Because men's souls are as violated as women's, and because they have fewer psychic resources for protest and support, men will often turn to violence because many of the roles awaiting them will violate their souls even more. Few boys today want to grow up and be like their dads. They have seen the cost of all that, so they delay growing up as long as they can. To "treat" those violated souls, they apply the medicaments of drugs, sex, booze, and a life of distraction. So many have self-rage, and sadly, as we all know, this often gets transferred to women.

7. *Every man carries a deep longing for his father and for his tribal fathers.*

Fathers too can love, care for, teach, and mentor their sons, but so few are able because they are the children of unmentored, unfathered dads as well. When men weep in therapy as they infrequently do, ninety percent of the time it is when they mention their lost, missing, depressed, angry dads. And then, surprised at this welling up of emotion, they usually apologize as if they have done something wrong. They have—they violated the code of silence and stumbled over perhaps their greatest longing and need, pushed aside, repressed and foreign to them as it may be.

8. *If men are to heal, they must activate within what they did not receive from without.*

Women cannot fix this mess. Only men can, and more and more men are realizing this, thus becoming better partners and dads. More and more recognize the need for male Eros, male friendship, male love, and something better than the competitive zero-sum game we inherited. More and more men now recognize talking about this in therapy, or with other males, is not a sign of weakness as we were conditioned to believe but an act of courage, and the first step to real freedom.

Several obvious points come from this brief survey of male conditioning. We do know that women are generally more comfortable sharing their difficult times with other women than men are with anyone else. Whether it is the accumulative effect of either nature or nurture—probably both, women are way out in front of most men in emotional intelligence, and capacity to share that with another. For men, the paradox is "Why would I share my weakness, my failure, my vulnerability with someone else? They might use it against me." It is not just paranoia on their part, but the residue of having been shamed in their formative histories, and probably more recently, for any hint of being less than a full man, whatever the Hell that is. For such men, the intimacy that therapy invites, the confessional nature of its discourse, is something men distrust, something already too "feminine" in its modality and its expectations. When U.S. gymnast Simone Biles withdrew from the intense pressure of the 2021 Tokyo Olympics, women and teammates leaped to her defense, for all of them knew the "twisties," the overwhelming anxiety that separates one from one's center. A high official in the state government of Texas, Biles' place of residence, quickly labeled her "a national disgrace." He may be a troglodyte in fact, but that clearly was the male world of win-at-all-costs, "there is no substitute for victory," in which he had been raised speaking through him. His macho world is one in which only winning is acceptable; all else is shameful. The more macho the man, or the culture, the greater the fear of the inner life, allied with an extreme sensitivity to shaming. This is why the deep secret of macho men is their utter terror of things "feminine." So great is that fear, they must even keep it from themselves.[17]

Most men, and I among them, are conditioned not only to be isolated from other men whom they are bred to distrust and defeat, but they are also profoundly estranged from themselves. (Remember my first dream in Zürich of being a knight defending a castle and the inner guide, the Anima, was a witch? How related was that dreamer at that time to his inner world?) It is also clear that given the self-estrangement of most men, how can they have genuinely reciprocal relationships with intimate partners whose very presence

---

[17] Recently, Lane Johnson, hulking tackle for my Philadelphia Eagles, shared his struggles with anxiety and his efforts at recovery. Such public courage will help other men take that risk.

activates this whole sordid history? Accordingly, they move to dominate that "other," or spend their life trying to please her—both are the residue of the unbalanced relationships of their history. Thus, the question is, how can one begin to be mindful of the immense hurt and storm inside of each man—a lake of tears and a mountain of anger—and begin to move him toward greater insight and personal liberation.

Just as I identified a few questions in the therapy of couples above that I hope are helpful in melting the frozen seas we carry within, here too I offer some questions to ask that man in therapy, or that man in your life. He may not like them; he may run from them; he may laugh at them or ridicule them; but something inside already knows and tells him, "They have you spotted. You are not really that guy you pretend to be." He is, of course, a recovering child, as are the women of this world, and desperately needs to hang on to the coping strategies of denial and belligerence that got him this far. But these improvised defenses are increasingly experienced as exhausted and ineffective. The capacity of women to face these threatening challenges to their assembled false self is why they are moving ahead in this hour of history. Many gay men are also way ahead of those timorous macho types. Men everywhere need to wake up, and someone needs to ask them these questions. After the flight, the denial, the tears, they may in fact, perhaps, someday, thank you...perhaps.

1. *What do you find most difficult in being a man?* This is such an obvious question, but believe it or not, most men have never thought about it. Certainly, they have not discussed it with other men. It's the opening probe into asking him to be more conscious about what he is *already* experiencing. Some men will be fairly agile here and respond with a good example, a joke to deflect the seriousness of this

invitation, and other men will ask you what you mean by that question. Be mindful of these sleights of hand to delay, fend off, and if possible avoid opening that door at all. Few will understand the question immediately.

2. When did you think you "shut down?" What caused that? They may ask you what do you mean "shut down," and you can safely respond: "At some point you were a happy, bubbly little child. And then somewhere, sometime, you learned that was dangerous, and you began to hide yourself from others, at least those most tender places of you. Was it before grade school? During grade school? Later?" And then follow up with the question of "And have you stayed in touch with those parts of yourself that you shut down, or have they been lost to you?" "Do you think that their recovery might be something good for you, even useful to you now?"

3. However you understand this word, whether you consider yourself as "religious" or not, do you think You have a Soul? And if so, what is it asking of you? I have asked this question of both men and women, and thus far, no one, no one, no matter how irreligious, no matter how secular they may consider themselves, has denied having a "soul." They may want to deny it through some disclaimer, or qualify its usage, but they all have some sense of deep values that matter to them. Those deep values are who they really think they are, even if they keep it hidden from others. And, perhaps surprisingly, most folks, when asked, have some answer to the question of what their soul is asking of them. They have been living with that for some time, even if they haven't made it very conscious, let alone a priority.

4. What did you most want from your father, and never got? Have you made that conscious, gotten angry at him, grieved him, forgiven him?

Most men are pretty distanced from that deep ache within. They hunger for the wise, helpful, mentor dad.

Many of them spend their lives looking for him out there somewhere, though they may not know what and for whom they search. Equally, they long for "wise fathers" to give them a larger story, wisdom for the journey, and even techniques to bear the sufferings that life brings each of us. This unhealed wound is critical to open because until he understands his bereavement and the many ways he runs from it, he will live a rootless life. Many men are angry at their father's betrayal, and the betrayal of the collective fathers. They do not want to become those men who often drink too much, or run from stepping into the question of "Who the Hell am I to be if not him?" They also need to come to a place, if they can, where they can remember that their fathers were other un-fathered sons, lost men in general, adrift in the materialist, competitive culture and wholly barred from the kind of information and permission increasingly available for men these days. If they can grieve their loss, and their father's lonely life, they can usually also reach forgiveness of him. Without this work, the Father complex remains a suppurating wound.

5. *What do you think will "heal" you? How do you go about obtaining that for yourself rather than expecting someone else to do that for you?* This is a loaded question, and they may not know what to do with that word "heal," but it is a necessary question. They all need to heal, and long for a clue as to how to go about that. And they, like many women, have long sought someone to make that happen. All men have carried this agenda, and all are surrounded by tons of clues as to healing within them for a very long time. But now is the hour in which addressing that agenda grows urgent. And for most, it means starting from the basics again, namely: what got left behind, what got suppressed.

6. *Where do you need to "grow up?"* We all know that holding power positions, wealth and status, access to

the instruments of cultural life, do not a grown-up make. Being a grown-up must, at the least, oblige a sense of total responsibility for our choices, their consequences, and for finding the courage to step into the perpetual demands life, and the soul, make of us. Any deferral of that responsibility, or deflection onto others, or numbing of the pain of forgetting the journey is living in Sartre's *mauvais foi*, bad faith. On my computer printer, I have this reminder from *The Odyssey*, "I will stay with it and endure. / through suffering hardships. / And once the heaving sea has shaken my raft to pieces / then will I swim." When forgetting is so easy, this reminds me each day not to whine, but to show up the best way I can. Odysseus was determined to survive the perils of the wine-dark sea, and as difficult at the outer opponents were, those of *fear* and *lethargy* within are even more threatening. Growing up requires that we recognize and contend with those twin foes day in and day out, as best we can. That is what life, that is what the soul, asks of us.

7. *What excites you, brings you joy, enthusiasm, a reason for living? And how can you bring more of that into your life?* The isolation of men from women, from other men, and from themselves, is profound, debilitating, and dangerous to all. Yet within, and out from under, the Saturnian weight of male role constrictions, his free, spontaneous soul still longs for release and for expression. Joy, enthusiasm, a story larger than our burdens—all are possible if a man can once again feel the freedom to let these aspirations rise from deep within him. These life-affirming affects are buried under tectonic layers of suppression, repression, and oppression, and yet like a gusher tapped by a wild-cat driller, they wish to burst into the surface of his life once again.

Doing therapy with men is a formidable task. It is virtually hopeless when he has a gun at his head, be it an angry spouse or a court order. (And I have had both in reluctant therapy.) He has to reach a point where he sees something there for him, rather than pleasing others, or resisting others, one more time. If he ever tumbles to the idea that he can have a richer life, he will commit to the process. To do that, one has to get around the denial, the defenses, and the intimidation of the journey.

It is my hope that these seven questions will open a door for him to walk through, perhaps to build a positive alliance with his therapist, and then, experiencing the reward of that psycho-spiritual enlargement, he may gradually be willing to take the next step and bring his richer selfhood into the world to share with his partner, his children, his comrades. This process, as with most healing, takes patience, time, and many risks, but the well-being of this world literally depends upon it.

III. Addressing Spiritual Naiveté and Immaturity

> "Doubt is not a pleasant condition, but certainty is
> an absurd one."
>
> Voltaire

As therapists we are supposed to be value neutral when it comes to matters political or religious, and for very good reasons. More than once I had to throttle my response in order that neither issue interfere with a client's process. I left a personal physician once, one I knew to be caring and competent, because he began to give me political tracts to take home. It didn't matter what I thought about those tracts; it did matter that a third, extraneous presence had entered our working space. While I haven't been wholly consistent—

our reactions to national events being hard to disguise—still a good faith effort in the direction of neutrality is certainly the goal. After all, the well-being of the client is more important than our agreement on such matters. A colleague in another city once expressed a good rule of thumb on these matters: "If you are not comfortable having your colleagues watching the decision you are making now, perhaps you should really reconsider and refrain." I have thought of that admonition many times, and it has proved very helpful to me.

All that said, in this essay I want to address where the issue of spirituality is critical to the work of not only helping a client move through the difficulties that brought them there, but grow and mature. Having a client who is a grown-up is often rarer than one might think.

You may know the old saying that "Religion is for those afraid of going to Hell; spirituality is for those who have already been there." If a therapeutic relationship is really going to be effective, it needs to enhance, if not sometimes, create, a more mature human being with whom to work. Children need comfort, protection, and guidance. Adults need to pull up their socks, stop whining, stop blaming, and take on the issues directly. Yes, some clients come hammered by life, in the dismal swamplands of the soul, but we must remember, as I demonstrated in the book *Swamplands of the Soul* three decades ago: *in every swampland there is a task, the addressing of which leads a person from victimage to active participation in the unfolding of their lives.* To get to that task, amid the miasma of misery we often encounter, we have to support, re-educate, and sometimes embody for clients what it means to be an adult, and what it will take for them to get there. This project arises from no paucity of compassion for suffering, but from an experiential perspective that has informed our journeys, and has brought us to a place where we can both empathize, analyze, and model a more integrated and a more mature approach to life.

I have often been stunned by what I will generically call an ill-considered "philosophy of life" that many clients bring to the table. To this end we therapists often ascribe the circumstances of their family of origin dynamics and/ or the traumatic vicissitudes of their childhoods as causal factors. However, I have increasingly come to believe that this psychological immaturity comes more and more from an adolescent pop culture in which we all swim. To my bill of indictment I would also like to add the noxious effect of such social media as *Facebook* and, further, really, really bad theology. So much of clients' modern religious exposure winds up infantilizing them by exploiting their parental complexes and making them stay powerless, guilt-ridden children, or seduces them with feel-good promises that quickly dissolve when reality arrives. (Both of these two aberrations, ironically, are the only two that have grown in adherents since World War II. Apparently, reiterating parentification patterns, or promising an easy road sell best.)

In reflecting on this all-too-common state of immaturity, I identify seven specific descriptors of a view of life that is infantile, unrealistic, and most importantly, contributes to the stuckness patients find in their lives. I am not suggesting that we make this list an overt agenda of confrontation, but I am suggesting that we pay attention and recognize these issues when they emerge, and that we challenge them in supportive and appropriate ways. Otherwise, unwittingly, we collude with their lack of spiritual preparation for the difficult times, and ratify their stuckness.

The seven beliefs/attitudes/ideas comprising an immature view of life are as follows:

1. *The Fantasy of Steady-State Happiness*

There are many folks out there, many, who are unhappy simply because they are unhappy much of the time. Can someone somewhere tell me where it is indelibly written that we are supposed to be happy? Oh yes, it is in the American *Declaration of Independence* that we are guaranteed life, liberty, and the pursuit of "happiness." But scholars of the eighteenth century have concluded that what Jefferson meant by that word in that era was the right to pursue a life of personal satisfaction, a life that mattered to that person rather than having it defined for them. Happiness is transient, contextual, and often outside our power to generate, no matter how hard we try. Happiness most occurs unexpectedly, unplanned in moments of encounter, or when we are in right relationship with ourselves, no matter how fraught the circumstances. I know folks who are unhappy because their friends on *Facebook* and other social media are deliriously happy with their children, or grand-children, or their vacations—or so they report. How many of those dear social media friends ever really report the reality:"Today, I messed up again, one more time when I knew better," or "I know my children don't want to visit but do because they feel duty bound, and besides, I let them know if they don't,"or "Well, Ralph and I got into another argument today. You know about what…." If truth in advertising were really enforceable, folks would stop these marketing reports about their steady state of bliss. And there are those good souls who really try to do the "right thing," whatever that is, and life keeps dumping on them. And because they are not "happy," they think their life a tragic mistake, and they the chief culprit. This notion of "happiness" is a pernicious, modern phantasy. Most of the history of humanity was a desperate struggle to survive, and happiness for them might have been a piece of bread or a night of untroubled sleep. Happiness is overrated because, surprise, it does not make us happy. It is the phantasy of happiness that makes most of us unhappy, most of the time.

2.   *We Can Find a Sanctuary, a Really Safe Place, Where We Are Protected from Harm*

It was natural for folks in the wilderness to bond and band together to find an alliance against marauding animals and other predators. It is natural to assume that apotropaic rituals will protect us from harm. Such rituals are our impositions of presumptive order upon an autonomous and unpredictable world out there. Sports and entertainers often have their rituals designed to bring good luck. When walking into diploma exams in Zürich many moons ago a German colleague whispered to me, *"Hals und Bein Bruch,"* "may you break your neck *and* your leg." (Those Germans are serious players, apparently.) We all develop our phantasies of security. Perhaps the most understandable—tracking back to the origins of human civilizations—is the petition to the gods for safe passage in this perilous world. I could start a long list of what so often befell those good souls that would break your heart, but the record of history is clear to anyone with the fortitude to examine it. One can use privilege, wealth, power to insulate oneself from the dirtiness of the world, but sooner or later, it finds a crevice, an opening to fell the most deluded of planers. So, too, many in our divided land move to geographical safe zones, or only listen to one news source, so as to offer them the pseudo-security of like-minded folks, with like-minded opinions. Our recent visitation by the micro virus of Covid reminds us that there is no *Citadel Unscalable*, no *Sanctuary Impervious* that is immune to the tiniest agents on the planet. Our vulnerability goes where we go. No matter how far we flee, it is there in the suitcase we open, having traveled with us. Anywhere, anytime, one's mortality is up for grabs. As novelist Thomas Hardy expressed it in his 1866 poem "Hap," meaning "happenstance, or fortuity,"

> How arrives it joy lies slain,
> And why unblooms the best hope ever sown?
> —Crass Casualty obstructs the sun and rain,
> And dicing Time for gladness casts a moan.

So much for sanctuary, and all those jury-rigged guarantees against the onslaught of time, tides, and the perversities of humankind.

3. *A Generalized Expectation That the Universe Is Fair*

Even those who have read *Job* or *Ecclesiastes* still expect that life will be "fair," that is, favor them in some way. Perhaps if life were really fair we all would be in even worse trouble than we are, given how we have lived, perhaps unintentionally, on the backs of those less fortunate, polluted this transient earth, and have generally not served the principle of "fairness" that well in our daily lives. Who among us is wise enough to say what is fair? Could we argue that the ultimate fairness is the democracy of death in that all of us wind up in the same place? Is the ego pleased with such a sense of fairness? John Kennedy once said, "Life is not fair." He said this in the context of sending off 10,000 more troops to Viet Nam. They, and he, had difficult appointments to keep. As we all do. Life "betrays" all of us we sometimes feel. Knocks us down when we are trying so hard to do "the right thing." But even doing the right thing, we can never fully foresee the consequences of our acts as they ripple down the line. Many great advances of the hour in time bring hardships and unforeseen consequences. It may not endear one to others to say, "stuff happens," or "shit happens," but it does, and our expectations otherwise so often are undermined by reality. e. e. cummings had this in mind when he extolls the flash and shazam of Buffalo Bill who dazzled his contemporaries, and then concludes in his poem "buffalo bill's defunct," "how do you like your blue-eyed boy, Mr. Death?" Or as novelist Kurt Vonnegut frequently observed, "so it goes."

4.   *We Project, and Expect, That Right Behavior on Our Part Will Lead to Reciprocity from Life Itself*

Nearly three millennia ago, an unknown Hebrew poet chose to critique the assumption of his people that they had a deal, a de facto "contract" with the universe. Borrowing a story from the region, the poet creates a monologue by Job, a right-acting, right-thinking soul. In fact, he is so righteous in his intent that he even superintends the piety of others. But a ton of woe falls on his head and devastates his life, his family, his world. Anguished, he seeks to summon God as his chief witness that he played by the rules, but when the Party of the First Part appears as a voice out of the whirlwind, he admonishes Job for his presumption that one can dictate a contract with the universe, and compel the Transcendent Other into compliance. In short, ain't no contract! But all of us from time to time have sought to effect "deals" with the universe, or so we believe. "If I do this or this, and don't do that or that, you will provide me safe passage—an A in math, my loved ones won't die, and life in general look upon me with favor...right?" Given that we established in the paragraph above that stuff happens, this "deal" proves ephemeral at best, and yet who among us stops trying to make such arrangements? Even folks who arrive at mid-life and who did what they were supposed to, often find themselves depressed, divorced, and dissolute, wondering what went wrong with the quid pro quo they presumed and upon which acted faithfully. Or those who did their best as parents, find their children make other decisions, follow a trajectory that was perhaps within them from the first, and leads them to quite troubled places. Or those who think eating all the right things, exercising, and so on will guarantee good health and longevity, may walk in front of a truck, or suddenly be confronted by a tumor with a mind of its own. The notion that we can make deals with the universe is older than the Job legend, but it never fully goes away. Educating ourselves and others to the fact that stuff happens is a beginning, and in every case we have a summons to identify a task which recovers greater psycho-spiritual integrity and dignity. Identifying and executing that task is what restores a sense of agency when we would otherwise wallow in victimage, rage, desuetude, or despair.

5.   *We Look Assiduously to Find Some Person, Program, or Ideology to Take Care of It for Us, Help Us Not Have to Grow Up and Deal*

If we ask ourselves what it means to be a "grown-up," it clearly demands more than a big body, and big roles, and big hair-dos. In fact, as we speak, children are impregnating each other and passing on the problems from their generation to the next. Being a grown-up means, essentially, that despite whatever formative things happened in my life, I am responsible for what spills into the world through me. I cannot just blame my personal parenting, however influential it might have been. I cannot blame ignorance. I cannot blame unconsciousness. In fact, Jung once said the unforgivable sin is to *choose* to remain unconscious. (For this tempting option, our present world offers many possible avenues.) Whatever happened, it is not what I am; and who I am is tracked with a responsibility for everything I do, or fail to do, and I am accountable for its reverberating consequences through the generations. Understandably, this may prove to be a heavy burden. Adults accept it as a reminder of the daily summons to interrogate our actions, or inactions, and hold ourselves accountable for them. The rest of the folks in big bodies run from this summons and continue the blunder, the damage, and reinforce the iron-clad rule that these issues will keep spilling into the world, their children, and the human family all around us. Our popular culture, already established as adolescent in its distractions, its binary thinking, its impatience to move on to the next slander, the next shiny thing, the next diversion, contributes to this general immaturity.

Inside each of us is a tremulous child who looks to find the "parent" figure, institution, ideology to address the questions and tasks of life. From them we hope to receive protective services, secret explanations and short-cuts, and, if really lucky, relief from the burden of growing up. This child within us often infantilizes our adult relationships, is drawn to attractive, well-coifed spiritual soap salesmen on the telly, and to simplistic truisms as abiding wisdom and guides for the perplexed. Real life is much more complex and demanding than that, but their simplifications, and deferrals of authority, are all the more appealing and seductive. Someone else can do the thinking for me. When Robert Frost wrote his well-known poem "Mending Wall," he was not recommending "good fences make good neighbors," as has been lifted out of context and so frequently quoted. Frost was smarter than that. He was critiquing the lazy habit of walling off the other, walling off differences, rather than engaging them and growing from them.

That child within is always peering out into the world and asking, "Who out there is going to explain this to me? Who out there is going to spare me the rigors of this journey?

Who out there is going to help me remain a child?" It is perfectly normal, even universal, for all of us to carry that "child within." But you would not let that child drive your car in heavy traffic, and so perhaps you should not let that child drive your life either.

6. *One's Imago Dei Is Childlike, Literalistic*

Most of us know that Freud's general dismissal of religion and spirituality as unexamined neurosis and infantilized projections was too dismissive. He had his own complexes around such matters. And we also understand that when one is trying to conceptualize the profundity of the Mystery in which we swim, we remain within our finite human categories at best, and fall back into familiar analogues such as the parent/child paradigm. But we all do still need to examine the assumptions we bring to our concepts, metaphors, practices and pass "the Freud test." Are my images, practices something more than mere projections of personal experience and longing onto the blank tablet of the universe? Do these images, practices keep me locked into childhood agendas and embody a surreptitious sleight of hand to avoid the difficult questions of life which arise from truly encountering the mystery of the Mystery?

Any view that causes us to over-simplify or finesse the raggedy margins of the Mystery says more about us than about the Mystery. Remember the old joke about the fellow being shown the Rorshach ink blots, "Why do you keep showing me these dirty pictures?" or it its variant, "How did you get all these pictures of my mother?" Our images are *our* images, and not the radical Other. They are all, perhaps unwittingly, confessional in character in their revelations of our stuck places, our hidden agendas, or our sneaky deals with the great unknown, what Luther called the *Deus Absconditus*.

123

Being a grown-up, see *supra*, means stepping into a mature position, one that respects the indefinable in life, one that cares enough about the complexity of truth to allow it to remain ungraspable by our limited brains and imaginations, one that can abide ambiguity and uncertainty. That these conditions are taxing to us is obvious, and hence the slippery deals and practices that characterize our species, but spiritual maturity means living in the midst of the unknowing, and still doing our best to be a free, and responsible person. It means we are now more clearly tasked with discerning our values, where they come from inside of us, and living them as faithfully as possible. There are no guarantees in life, but one still has to risk living it. There are seldom certainties, but one still has to make choices every day. What part us makes those choices, the child or the adult?

7.   *We All Look for Someone to Tell Us the Big Picture, Sort It All Out for Us*

Wherever we are uncertain and look for answers, we can be assured that there are plenty of folks out there perfectly willing to tell us what to think, feel, and how to behave. The bookstores are full of "self-help" books with easy lessons and thirty-day results guaranteed. If they worked, we would only need one book. And the street corners and t.v. channels are filled with would-be prophets and purveyors of suspect spiritual goods who offer certainties, answers to life's thorny questions, and of course expect you to leave some tokens of appreciation in their collection trays. We all know life is much more demanding, more elusive than these simplistic entreaties. This is why my books speak to some folks, and turn off many others. I consistently try to leave the mystery open, encourage personal accountability, and occasionally offer a tool that might be helpful along life's highway. It may not be much, but it is what I have to offer. Good luck with looking elsewhere.

Given the unexamined immaturities I have identified above, it is natural that the child within, or the intimidated adult, will look to a guru out there, an authority of some kind, given that one traded away one's personal authority a long time ago. This is why the recovery of personal authority, namely, sorting through the incessant bombardment from the exterior world, and the immense traffic within, to find the voice of our own soul is so necessary. If we don't make a sustained, good-faith effort to find that voice, we will be obeying the noisiest demand from the environment of the hour, or be a slave to our autonomous complexes that will run our life for us. There is no one out there, NO ONE, who knows, and those who might know at least something, are mostly silent. So, growing up requires beginning to trust one's own internal apparatus for clues as to which path is right for us. Only in this effort can we gain a greater purchase on our journeys. The alternative is to be imitating someone else's journey, or running from their example. (This is why Jung advised Christians not to literalize the *imitatio Christi*, for that had already been done, but rather to live their lives as fully as Jesus lived his.)The simple question is, "If I don't live *this* life, the one I have now, according to my inner lights, why am I here in the first place?"

So now it is incumbent on us perhaps to define a more mature spirituality, or philosophy of life, as the reader may prefer.

Possibly our most immediate aperture into this realm is to ask *what truly quickens the spirit*. Well, fear does for one thing, and touching a live wire also. But there are other experiences that touch and move our souls, and quicken the spirit. One way to look at this is to recall the concept of the *numinous*. The etymology of numinous suggests that something outside us nods or beckons us, and that summons

125

catalyzes the spirit within us. We are "quickened" by a certain piece of music, and not others; we respond to one painting or another; we delight in one experience and are blah in another. What is unique to each of us is the means by which the numinous arrives on our doorstep, and of course, whatever configuration of our interior matrix is such that responds to that stimulus.

But to talk of a "mature vs. immature" spirituality is to raise the necessary question of "Who says so," and "What are those criteria?" When we are newborns, we have a guiding authority; it is called instinct. But as we have demonstrated, that link to our guiding source is quickly overrun, even effaced, by the incessant demands of the world around us. Again, this brings us to the dilemma regarding the recovery of "personal authority" in the later decades of one's life. *What is true for you? What not? Why do you say that? How do you know? And now, are you prepared to live your truth in this world with its consequences, or prepared to live the consequences of your continued evasions of your personal truth?*

When therapists work analytically helping to separate the analysand from their psychic enmeshment from the parental field of influence, it is important to recall those strange words of the itinerant rabbi Jesus who said, "Who is with Mother and Father is not with me." (*Matthew*, 10:37) Or, when he saw his mother at the marriage at Cana, "Woman, what hast thou to do with me?" Was he expressing a strong mother complex and in need of analysis, or did he intuitively understand the need to leave received authority in search of one's own, authentically lived journey?

In working with individuals in the context of the post-modern world, and in the barrage of stimuli in which we all drown each day, I have come to this conclusion: *If we do not experience the numinous within, amid the many cacophonous claims upon us, it will come to possess us through our projections of it onto the secular world, or turn inward as malady and percolate to the surface later through our symptomatology.*

In the first instance, materialism, the filling of the abyss within with the latest of the latest from the world of material shiny things, is a national mania. In the latter, deeply unmet needs become addictions, or autonomous anxiety management rituals and avoidances. Accordingly, if the life of the spirit is not nourished, it will pathologize, or as Jung once observed, the gods will enter the solar plexus of the modern and become diseases. He also noted that our actual spiritual investments are less tied to a creed or confession or institutional affiliation than we might intend, but are really found where our energy is most utilized on a daily basis. When we make that kind of critical analysis, we find that the maintenance of our neuroses, and their protections against whatever goes bump in the night for us, constitute our de facto religious affiliations. This fact explains why so many in our land embrace political figures and political policies that directly contradict the tenets of their faiths. In short, they are owned by their complexes, their fears, and their searches for apotropaic "fixes" for the new world that has arrived. This is not really religion or spirituality; it is psychopathology on parade with fears and stuck places calling the shots. Those who deny the accumulated knowledge of our species, who ignore the findings of modern medicine, astronomy, physics and so on, and those who shun self-examination at every moment, live in a world of denial, "confirmation bias," and an ever-diminishing spiritual horizon. Their gods hate the same people they hate; their catechisms collaborate and conspire with their complexes; and their understanding of self and world as "other" is manipulated into a conformity with their fear-based agenda, resistance to change and ambiguity, a reflexive prizing of certainty over complexity, and reassurance over the central thrust of primordial religious encounter: wonder.

A brief note on the difference between phenomenon and epiphenomenon might prove useful here. When people encounter the numinous, whether a burning bush or the smile of their beloved, they have a felt experience, and in some way transformative encounter. But how does one hang on to that experience which is in many ways outside the realm of consciousness? When we have such experiences, images emerge and present themselves to consciousness. Since we can't hang on to that autonomous energy of the experience, we grab hold of that image in an understandable effort to fix it, hold it, make it ours. But the image is not the phenomenon; it is the epiphenomenon, a secondary byproduct of primal experience. Thus people will wind up worshiping the image rather than whatever mystery gave rise to that image. This is the oldest of religious sins: idolatry, fixating on the image, rather than the transcendent dynamism that energized the image. Thus people wind up worshiping the relic, the husk perhaps, long after the energy has departed. Many folks are more in love with the image of love than those who actually love. Some are more in love with their phantasy of marriage than their human partners.

Any encounter with the numinous can bring us into the precincts of mystery. Jung put it this way:

> "It is only through the psyche that we can establish that God acts upon us, but we are unable to distinguish whether these actions emanate from God or from the unconscious. We cannot tell

whether God and the unconscious are two different entities.

Both are border-line concepts for transcendental contents. But empirically it can be established, with a sufficient degree of probability, that there is in the unconscious an archetype of wholeness. Strictly speaking, the God-image does not coincide with the unconscious as such, but with this special content of it, namely the archetype of the Self."

By "Self," Jung of course does not mean the ego. The Self is the organic and organizing energy that drives our lives. It is both vehicle, energy, and purpose. The self is teleological; it moves us through the phases of our journey from zygote to ghost. It carries us, nudges us, and opposes us when it is oppressed.

Whatever the mystery may be "out there," we experience it "in here," and therefore our appreciation of spiritual life must include an appreciation for depth psychology, that branch of learning and practice which seeks dialogue with the unknown, which undertakes a conversation with the unconscious, and slowly begins to read and track and value the movement of the invisible energies as they course through the visible forms of the world. This is not to say that such encounters are "only psychological." They are not, but we can only experience them in concert with our psychological history, limitations, and complexes through which all such experiences are strained and reconfigured.

Assuming that the seven issues listed above are addressed, then one must counter with these five tests of, or characteristics of, a mature spirituality or philosophy of life.

1. *The Principle of Resonance*

When the outer encounter gives rise to our inner experience of the numinous, we resonate. We re-sound;

it reverberates; we hum; the tuning fork within vibrates. If you see a particular arrangement of pigments on a canvas, or hear the Delta blues, or enter the dark night of the soul, you are stricken; you are seized; you hum; you re-sonate. Someone else, with a similar experience is untouched. One has encountered the numinous; one has not. We may have a numinous experience, but we cannot transmit it to another. This is one of the frustrations of parents who want to pass on their tastes, politics, and values to their children. But their children have separate matrices within and are, or are not, moved, resonate or do not. Children may conform to those transmitted expectations out of compliance, but they do not experience resonance. Therefore, it remains someone else's experience.

I find it puzzling and problematic that so many institutions of good intent, be they religious organizations or universities, try to pass on experiences rather than seek to open "the doors of perception," to use Blake's phrase, so that their members can experience for themselves. As a former graduate student and professor, I shudder at how I initially sought to replicate my experiences in my students. Sometimes it worked in spite of me, but probably not that often. Rather, today I would try to approach the hope of engagement with the numinous in a different way.

In the end, if something resonates for us, it is true for us, at least for that moment. If we try to imitate the experience of others, we are likely to be left with the husk, the merely conscious, rather than the invisibly transformative encounter. The real question persists: is the spirit truly quickened here? Jung once wrote that without the quickening of the spirit humankind will slip back into indolence, the torpor of the unchallenged soul.

2. *Learn to Trust the Reality of One's Own Experience*

The problem of transmitting the experience of the numinous to another is insufficiently addressed psychologically, and therefore parents and organizations tend to depend on consensus and peer expectations. How many members of how many congregations actually feel the quickened spirit? Jung talked about how disappointed he was, dumbfounded even, when he went through his baptism as expected by his family and felt no quickening. Was he "wrong?" Of course not. The power of that ritual is significant: the return to the source, the primal waters of the womb, symbolically bespeaking if not always begetting a rebirth of one's psychospiritual view. For some it works; for others it does not. Which are right? A foolish question, and yet one unasked as generations suffer inculcation without access to the mystery. And what if they did? Many of them might very well choose a path different than their elders' wish for them. This is why some institutional figures are terrified that their congregants might actually have transformative religious experiences, or students might have transformative educational experiences. They might go off the reservation. I was proud when a former faculty body with whom I served many years ago gave each incoming student a tee shirt that said: "*Question Authority.*" I am sure for many of those students, this was the first time the idea had occurred to them, and perhaps the first time they found their elders willing to dialogue about authority.

When we are born, we trust *our* authority: we cry when hungry, excrete when surfeited, and sleep when it's just all too much to handle. But later, we all feel out-numbered, out-voted, and we silently fall in line with the group. I remember specifically thinking, probably around ten years old, "This does not make sense to me at all, but I am just a kid; and they are the big people, so they must be right." They weren't, but I didn't trust the reality of my experience then—and later had to learn the hard way to do so. Most of the adults I have seen in therapy are learning the hard way also. The Danish existential philosopher Kierkegaard said, "The crowd is untruth," and Jung added that the larger the group, the lower the level of consciousness. Still, out-numbered, out-voted, we capitulate and march to the tune of someone else's drummer. Sooner or later, whatever is true for us, whatever really resonates must be served, or something within sickens and sours, and life never feels right.

3. *Understand That One Can Only Embrace the Mystery through Verbs, not Nouns*

No one I know collects used light-bulbs, perhaps mounting them above a fireplace or next to one's place of repose. Why would one keep that glass and metal shell when the light has gone out of it? And yet, humans hang on to the old gods, sometimes for centuries, long after the light has gone out of them. Let me explain that later.

The moment we turn energies into nouns, we falsify them. When Jung asked where the gods of the antique world went, he concluded those energies departed, leaving only husks for consciousness to fasten onto. What is "divine," so to speak, is the energy not the husk. Teilhard de Chardin once suggested that matter is "spirit slowed enough to be seen." The gods then are archetypal energies slowed enough to be felt. Archetypes are formative energies not contents. Contents vary from context to context. They never really go away; they become invisible for a while and reappear with new names and new identities. It is ironic that we, the most fleeting, seek to hang on to the most transcendent of energies. In so doing, we serve our neuroses but not the essential mystery of life.

A client of mine, nearing his eighties, felt it important to return to the religion of his childhood to see if there was any spark left there for him. As part of this effort, he attended a Bible study group which wound up giving him more questions than answers. Later that night he dreamt that he was back in that group and asserts to his cohort that Divinity is found in the current that generates the light and not the container of the light. Other members are dismayed and deny his insight, and yet his dream got it exactly right. No one I know collects light bulbs after the luminous capacity has left them. We are briefly illumined, and then what is left is the glass receptacle not light.

Understanding this distinction is the premise of both depth psychology and a truly open theology. Both try to track the movement and motive of the elusive energy even as the ego prefers the more accessible concepts, reified, and hardened into signs. Symbols point beyond themselves to the mystery; signs carry an assigned meaning. The meaning may or may not persuade the mind, but it seldom touches the heart. Only the acausal energy of the autonomous Other does that.

Most people's ideas of Divinity or an afterlife are objectified as concepts, nouns, and whenever the facts or contrary experiences challenge the authority of those constructs, the whole enterprise grows shaky. Thus enters fundamentalism and dogmatism, both of which refuse to acknowledge that the energy has departed, and they are left with the enervated vitality of mere concepts. As my cleric friend Larue Owen asserts, "Insistence upon certainty produces toxic theology." Felt experience in the moment of experiencing is non-definable, and whatever follows is the epiphenomenon that seeks to catch hold and retain it. Nouns reify the energies into icons; verbs quicken the spirit. Hanging on to the husk after the energy has left is like saving spent light bulbs, or as they used to say of those who embraced the image rather than that to which it pointed, "idolatry."

4. *Accept That We Are Summoned to Grow Up, at Last Grow Up*

Neither the gods nor the animal kingdom makes theologies; humans do. Part of that enterprise is to understand, and part of it may well be the effort to exert some form of control over what we really *don't* understand. Many psychologies and even more theologies tell us more about the sensibility of the humans who espouse them than the mysteries. In fact, one of the reasons we study the foundational myths, rites, and literatures of other peoples is to reconstruct their inner topography, their values, and their complexes. Such primal *materia* becomes a revealing Rorschach for anthropologists and students of myth and depth psychology. Any religious practice and any psychological school should first provide entrée to and lead one deeper into the mystery of being human rather than box it in with what Alfred North Whitehead called "the bloodless dance of categories." And secondly, such practices should progressively summon maturation which moves us from dependency and intimidation to adulthood. Literal tales and parentifying institutions are for children, however old they may be. Understanding the practical wisdom or spiritual insight behind such tales and practices is something which can deepen and enhance the adult's journey. Jungian colleague Aldo Carantenuto once wrote in *The Difficult Art*,

> The ultimate purpose of psychotherapy is not so much the archeological exploration of infantile sentiments as it is learning gradually and with much effort to accept our own limits and to carry the weight of suffering on our own shoulders for

the rest of our lives. Psychological work {and truly insightful theology}, instead of providing liberation from the cause of serious discomfort increases it, teaching the patient to become adult, and for the first time in his life, actively face the feeling of being alone with his pain and abandoned by the world.[18]

Well, we can see why such views are never very popular. But the number of people who need comfort is far exceeded by the number of folks who need to be awakened, and challenged to grow up.

5. *Finally, Any Mature Philosophy of Life, or Mature Spirituality Will Lead Us Away from Security into the Realm of Mystery*

Just as a mature psychology of life will ask of us, a mature spirituality will be measured by our capacity to tolerate and function within what I call the *Triple A's*: ambiguity, ambivalence, and anxiety. Any one or all of them will trigger in us the desire to squelch unpleasant emotions in service to our management of them. But it is this understandable tendency that leads us to over-simplification, slanting the truths we encounter, denying contradictions, and finessing the unanswered. Such behaviors lead once again to self-delusion not to revelation and certainly not to spiritual growth. Our egos, not to mention a noisy choir of complexes, are rendered anxious by ambiguity and ambivalence, and therefore we often come down hard on the side of denial, simplification, and falsification. When is the good the enemy of the better? I once saw the Dalai Lama embody the open maturity to which we need aspire. When asked what he would do with his cherished beliefs if he found some of them

---

[18] Carentenuto, *The Difficult Art: A Critical Discourse on Psychotherapy*, p. 54.

contradicted by credible scientific evidence, he replied, "Why then I would change my beliefs." How marvelous! He is neither attached to, nor bound by, nor saddled with dogmas that cannot be challenged by something even more compelling.[19]

The human animal is easily duped by many things, even its own constructs. Indeed, we fall in love with our construings of the world and make monuments and cathedrals to them. Yet, as theologian Kierkegaard once observed, the god that can be named is not God, and Paul Tillich added that God is the God that appears out from behind the image of the god that just disappeared. That is, when we view the mystery as the unfolding of, and the movement of, both transcendent and immanent energy—and just when we think we have it—then it will leave this image, concept, practice, and transform into something else. The question is whether the human animal can be psychospiritually open enough to follow that energy to the new place in which it is invested, and to experience wonder or terror there.

Beware of seeking "religious" experience. You might get one. And what if that experience calls much of what the ego's five-year plan had in mind into question? The only way to live with the mystery in which we swim in good faith is to respect it as mystery. If my poor little brain and stunted imagination thinks it can own the mystery, then I am in a transient psychosis. When he concluded his 1937 Terry Lectures at Yale University, Jung said, "No one can know what the ultimate things are. We must take them as we experience them, and if such experience helps to make life healthier, more beautiful, more complete and more

---

[19] Similarly, Bertrand Russell once observed that he would not die for a cause or a belief "because I might be wrong."

satisfactory to yourself and to those you love, you may safely say: this was the grace of God."[20]

Remembering Jung's admonition that we cannot take our clients or congregants any further than we have traveled, it then falls to each of us to examine our beliefs, or non-belief beliefs, and ask: from whence have they come? Are they the product of my felt, resonant experience? What are they in service to: maintaining my security needs, or opening me to *wonder at the great mystery of all things*?

---

[20] Jung, *CW 11, Psychology and Religion*, para. 167

CHAPTER SEVEN

Living in Haunted Houses: The Latest News from the Madding Crowd Within

We are reminded of the profound gift Jung gave us with the recognition of the "complex," asking of us a re-collection of the invisible host of personages we all carry within. There are more folks within us, so to speak, than we have ever met in the external world. For those of you who have read about complexes in my other books, please skip this chapter, unless you have been in a complex recently and need a refresher, or reading this book has put you in one.

Nothing is more rare in any man than an act of his own.... Most people are other people.

Oscar Wilde

Our ancestors often believed in ghosts, revenants, states of possession, and other spectral interferences. Since these experiences were remote from consciousness, often contrary to the overt intentions of the ego, it made some sort of sense to see their imposition as coming from occult or recondite sources. "Since I did not intend this outcome," the reasoning goes, "it must be some alien presence that interfered with me." The initial sentence in the book *Hauntings: Dispelling* the Ghosts Who Run Our Lives reads, "We all live in haunted houses...." I chose that metaphor to suggest the recurrent truth that the past is never wholly past, and that that there are charged clusters of history operating in all of us at all times. Sometimes the manifestation of that energy is helpful to us, and sometimes pernicious. There is not an analytic hour in which I do not reflect some moment on the idea of complexes, namely, what intra-psychic field of energy is constellated and moving in the space between client and analyst. If I fail to think of it, it may be because I am captive to one of those presences, and know it not.

When Jung left the medical school at Basle at the beginning of the last century, he was first employed at the premier psychiatric facility in Switzerland, the Burghölzli Hospital in Zürich. Under the tutelage of Director Eugen Bleuler, a pioneer in modern psychiatry, nosology, diagnosis, and the creator of the term "schizophrenia," Jung was assigned research with the so-called Word Association Experiment which had arrived from Germany via Wilhelm Wundt and others. In this "experiment," a subject is given a series of words, ordinary words really, and then one observes the reaction of the subject. We are all familiar with the idea of the experiment. (It is called an "experiment" because it is open-ended. There are no "right" reactions. There are only the reactions of individuals in any given situation.) From his observations of so-called normal subjects, Jung identified over a dozen "disturbances of consciousness," that is, bodily movements, pauses, forgetfulness, and so on, that indicated that something within had been triggered in the person and produced an interference to their conscious flow of thought.

Quite separately, Jung had written his medical thesis on his investigation of a medium, a young woman who entered into a somnambulant state and quickly became the vehicle of "voices" that to observers seemed to embody the voices, intonations, and personalities of the departed. He asked himself if she was a fraud, not revealing that she was a relative whom he knew and trusted, or if she was psychotic, when clearly she was not. But what possible conclusion is left, if one is skeptical about the capacity of a living person to summon up the presence of the deceased? He reasoned that her ego was very labile, that is, fluid, permeable, and that she could suspend her conscious will, slip into a trance-state, and then these disparate parts of her psyche had free range to express themselves through her. The "I" we "know," and believe is who we are, is, quite simply, the ego's fluctuating capacity to reflect upon itself. What the ego does not know is how many fractionated selves may also be part of the psychodrama. The ego's limited imagination seems incapable of conjuring with the vast panoply of "others" that we also are, autonomous energy packets that move invisibly through our bodies, dreams, and our histories. (Jung noted, for example, that in dreams we are the observer, the stage, the audience, and all of the characters, even if we don't like some of them.)

In the last decade of the nineteenth century, Berlin psychiatrist Theodore Ziehen, also exploring the Word Association Experiment, coined the term *complex* (*Komplex* in German). As a word, it is neutral, but it is a cluster of energy that can be activated either by external stimuli, or internally by the stirrings of our psyche, and produces a bodily change, a reconfiguration of consciousness, and often a concomitant behavior. Jung recognized the richness of this concept and went on to revolutionize modern psychology.

Who among us has not used this term, without perhaps understanding what it means? I consider his emphasis on the complex to be perhaps Jung's most practical contribution to the practice of psychotherapy. Asking ourselves to what complexes is a person in service begins the forensic task of unloading that history. So, what, in fact, is a *complex*, as Jung described it?

In chapter 3 above we spoke of the importance of Jung's insistence on the centrality of the complex, the provisional "storying" of our past through which we see the new moment. Freud similarly talked about these disturbances of consciousness in his 1904 *The Psychopathology of Everyday Life*. In that work he posited that we don't have to visit an asylum to see the recrudescence of the unconscious, but we find it in our dreams, our forgetfulness, our slips of the tongue, our avoidances of painful subjects, and so on. Later he even gave Jung credit for developing the centrality of the complex as a determinant in much of our behavior, and for a while the Zürich analytic school was identified as "Complex Psychology."

Imagine, if you will, a clock face before you. At high noon, a stimulus confronts you. At three o'clock, the psyche is busy doing its data search, combing through extensive files of our history asking such questions as—"what does this mean,""what do we know about it," "is it friend or foe?" At six o'clock, the unconscious storehouse of history, the timeless thesaurus within, selects a file of some sort which carries whatever information is available on that particular cluster of history. At nine o'clock, the body is charged; a lens falls over the eyes for a moment; we see the present moment through the optics of the past, and a behavior follows, based on the strategy outlined in the file produced by the data search. Many times that dusty file is helpful: "beware here," "duck, that ball is coming at your head," "be prepared to fight," and so on. Many times that file is also prejudicial for the simple reason that it imposes on the present—a situation unique in our history—the lens, the interpretation, and the behavorial response associated with the past. For this reason, we might imagine swirls of energy in our wake, trailing out behind us like those tumbling constellations in Van Gogh's "Starry Night," landing upon the present, and adding another replicative layer to our patterned behaviors. Those patterns are there because they are generated by predisposed enactments of the script that dusty file sent up from below. So, just as we have multiple characters within, so we have many scripts for them.

Jung called these affect-laden energies "splinter personalities." Once I had a client who, when she grasped the richness of this way of mapping the unconscious, returned the next week with a whole catalogue of inner characters: "the teacher's pet," "the evasive politician," "the seductive naïf," and so on. I knew her prognosis was good because she grasped this gift of being able to consciously personify these energy systems within. Those who cannot will be living those personifications of history unconsciously. Another client often began her session with the sentence, "Let me tell you what the kids have been doing this week." I loved her narrative powers, too, for she further understood how most of the powerful unbidden visitants to her conscious life came from an early time in her development. Having that narrative understanding makes the work of self-awareness come alive, and gives consciousness a purchase on firmer ground for differentiation, and for engaging in a dialogue with these familiars. Only when we can name them, or identify their presence, do we have a chance of living in a conscious way. Much of the time, perhaps most of the time, we are carried along by these visitants, and serve their archaic agendas, whether we know it or not.

One might further characterize a complex as "an emotionally-charged reflex" for quanta of feeling are always attached to the moment. Given that their appearance is virtually reflexive in character, we ask ourselves, "How can we prevent them?" We can't, because we carry our history with us, and lumber through our allotted time carrying history on our back like those Galapagos turtles. "How can I know I am in a complex, then?" Well, that is a more approachable subject. Because there is always an epiphenomenal experience in the body, we may begin to recognize certain somatic changes. We perspire in the middle of winter; limbs stiffen; we feel nausea in the pit of our stomach; we feel the constriction of the throat, and so on. Each of us has familiar places where this complex-driven energy will manifest. Knowing, mapping, paying more attention, may often lead us to recognize we have entered that altered state sooner and begin to pull our way out of it.

Similarly, whenever a complex is triggered, it brings a rush of energy to the moment in excess of the rational requirements of the moment. The problem is, when one is in a complex, one readily adjusts one's rational framing to legitimize the energy level. This is why we often wonder why we froze the day before in the face of conflict, or were possessed by anger, and felt righteous in its service. Road rage is a classic illustration of how a complex can lead to an excessive response, and often very sad outcomes. It's not that one was just cut off in traffic—that happens in normal flow of give and take. It's because at that particular moment, a complex beneath the surface is activated, and up comes a message such as: "There they go again. They never respect you. Are you going to let them get away with that?" Thus some historic grievances add their weight to the moment, and the archaic energy flares forth into the present. The "they" of history gets transferred to the new moment, the new person in one's way, and this momentous invitation to finally redress the simmering grievance.

We will all recall childhood fears that dominated our lives and then fell by the wayside as we grew up. Most of us were afraid to be called on to speak in class, and probably all of us remember at least one occasion where it didn't go well when we were. That complex is likely to linger throughout our lives. Although I have taught at the university level or above for fifty-seven years now, and spoken publicly hundreds and hundreds of times, I always feel nauseous and neurasthenic beforehand. After all these years. But, I also know that something more important is at stake than childhood and family fears. If I am going to lay claim to my journey, serve the purposes that make sense to me, how can I not then push through those fears and do the best I can? It is worse to give in to those intimidating complexes than to go through them. It does help to understand that they are ephemera, clusters of archaic history with no more substance than the gossamer threads of a spider's web. For all their threat, the present hour is always reclaimed by "going through" the web rather than halting before it. This is why Jung observed that we do not "solve" these complexes of history, for history is carried in our neurology and our psyches, but we can grow larger than their reductive and regressive plans for us. Growing through them is perhaps what it means to become a grown-up. We have a history, a psychoactive history which travels wherever we travel, but we need not always be owned by it.

Mapping out our complexes is central to recovering an ownership of our lives. The sooner we are able to identify their recrudescence, the sooner we begin to regain a purchase in the present. And sooner or later, we will have to face the contretemps stirred within us, the antagonism between the various claims of the past and the immanent urgency of the present upon us. We can never lay claim to conscious conduct without tilting the balance to the present hour, thereby reframing our journey, with its more capacious choices than the iron padlocks of history ever permit. Without that conscious clarity, and, struggle, we remain locked in prisons we know not we are in. Jung's work has opened the door of many a cell for many a person.

CHAPTER EIGHT

The Gift, and the Limitations, of Therapy

This chapter is a reframing of the common expectations for therapy. Mindful of its many gifts, one must also realize that the paramount goal of therapy is to return ownership of life back to the patient to see what can be done with it. Therapy often fails, or people don't even undertake the effort, because of misunderstandings. And sometimes those who do understand want no part of it. For them we have drugs, alcohol, and a numbing popular culture as a ready alternative.

I certainly never expected to be in therapy. As a male, I thought, stupidly of course, that it all came down to will. If we willed enough, worked hard enough at it, things would sort out. The day I had my first therapy session at age thirty-five, long ago in Philadelphia, it certainly did not seem like the beginning of the second half of life. It felt like a massive defeat. And it was; it was the defeat of all my stupid assumptions. Ironically, unless something fails, or really falls apart, why would we ever want to challenge our adjustments to life, cast aside our defenses, reconfigure our priorities, and go back to the drawing board?

Before we get to the heart of the subject here, let us take a parenthetical break. There are many forms of therapy for many forms of problems: long and short term, talk, behavioral, cognitive, pharmacological, and so on. And there should be for we come to such a moment in our lives for many reasons with many different capacities in many different contexts. (Long ago, William James, in his 1902 *The Varieties of Religious Experience* celebrated rather than critiqued the many, many denominations and spiritual traditions, precisely because the conditions of life and variegated human needs and capacities were better served by this abundance of choices.) There are longitudinal studies which report the effectiveness or lack thereof for most of them if the reader wishes to look them up on-line. In this essay, I am not discussing the gifts and limitations of any of them other than the process known as talk therapy, and more specifically analytic therapy. Knowing that many folks cannot afford the time or the money for long-term therapy, I acknowledge those realities from the beginning, and lament those limitations. Nonetheless, for most psychospiritual issues not biologically driven, and a few that are, long-term talk therapy proves to be the most efficacious, as several longitudinal studies support. Now, back to our inquiry.

Many times one wants to find a new approach to the common problems of life: loss of energy, relational conflicts, stuckness, or career malaise. All of these problems are the stuff of daily life, and one moves through them somehow, remains mired in them, or one finds a new attitude in addressing them. It is also true that those old clichés, the presence of maternal and paternal imagoes, do need to be excavated and brought into the light of day. This work can be the work of a lifetime, for Mumsy and Dada never really leave one's psychic caverns. Who could ever forget those famous words of England's Philip Larkin in his 1971 "This Be the Verse,"

They fuck you up, your mum and dad.
They may not mean to, but they do.
They fill you with the faults they had
And add some extra, just for you.

He goes on to remind us that they were someone else's children as well. We repeat their lives, their messages, run from them, or are unwittingly trying to solve it all through some unconscious strategies. But to step out, finally, from under the umbrella of their exempla, their messages, their limitations, into the open air of one's own journey is no small accomplishment.

As suggested in the essay above regarding the rather common philosophic or spiritual immaturity of our time, stepping into the total responsibility for one's life is profoundly intimidating, but ultimately freeing. No whining allowed. As Jung put it, "People will do anything, no matter how absurd, in order to avoid facing their own souls. They will practice Indian yoga and all its exercises, observe a strict regimen of diet, learn the literature of the whole world— all because they cannot get on with themselves and have not the slightest faith that anything useful could ever come out of their own souls." Of course, Jung has nothing against yoga, diet, and learning, quite the contrary. He is rather asking us where we might be substituting a good of some kind in avoiding the better.

His last phrase is compelling and stunning in its way, that we "have not the slightest faith that anything useful could ever come out of our own souls." The notion that our own souls may be the source of our future healing and guidance is still a radical thought, even a presumption that could only be verified by the leap into that possibility. As we have noted repeatedly, our faith in our own resources is diminished by the intimidation of the large, noisy, demanding world all around us, and by the necessary adaptations to it. That we might be self-healing organisms is still a revelation to most of us. I recall taking our dog Shadrach to the vet for surgery. When I went to bring him home, I asked the doctor when I might let him up to walk around. He looked at me incredulously: "He's a dog; he'll tell you when." I learned something obvious, and profound, then. Nature knows. I learned, and am still learning, how we are in fact flush with clues, promptings, and correctives from our nature all the while, even when distracted, productive in the outer world, and leading a "successful" life.

While discussed in the initial essays of this book, let me briefly review such indices we all carry because for most readers this will be new, if oh so familiar at the same time. First of all, we have to recall, and even be grateful for, the autonomy of the psyche. Not only could we never manage all the complex systems the human relies upon minute to minute, but we could not even know what was right for this organism, given that we are so adaptive to the pressures of the hour.

First in line for such indications that we are off course, misaligned, is psychopathology itself. While all our medications and most of our therapeutic approaches seek the reduction of symptoms immediately, we have to rather inquire why they have arrived, to what are they reacting, and even more deeply: what might the psyche wish instead? Whether it is anxiety or depression or some failing treatment plan we have devised, the psyche is calling our cards, and challenging our choices. What does the psyche (soul) want is the last question we are likely to ask for such an interrogatory leads the ego to a long-resisted invitation to submission rather than conquest. In other words, we will have to abandon our previous modus operandi for something that raises even more discomfort. No wonder we fight growth and change as we have seen. If our defense does not work for us, how then are we to move forward? This quandary is the same as that which is faced in the first step of the Twelve Step programs: "Your present management system has failed, and you are going to have to find a way to live without that. Think you can handle that?"

Secondly, the feeling function renders a qualitative judgement about how matters are being conducted even before consciousness is allowed to consult it. Again, we may deny, repress, suppress, project, or drug that feeling, but it has already happened. The animalia have fled the barn, and how will the bewildered ego stuff them all back in? Thirdly, our dreams regularly address our fears, our stuck places, our projections, and lift the forgotten agendas into prominence. We may have difficulty making sense of them for dream work is an art and not a science, but it does repay our efforts as we allow the thaumaturgical images to percolate and brew until we begin to grasp their import for us. Those who have had a dream open up a puzzle for them, or tell them what they knew but were afraid to acknowledge, begin to change. They have to because they now know that something inside now grows more and more important to them. From that point onward, they have to reckon with the fact that something within them, some agency, some wisdom knows them better than they know themselves. Those who think they know themselves through the acts of ratiocination, or even careful, conscious minding of the store, as I once believed, are simply charmed, bewitched by their ego's own insistence on its sovereignty. Not only do we not by definition know the unconscious, the vast sea within, but most of the time we do not even know what complex has occupied the ego nor through what refractive lens the ego sees and construes the world at that instant.

Fourthly, our energy systems confirm or deny where the ego is making its investments. The harsh demands of reality force all of us to deal with what life brings us, not what we wish but with what happens. But if we, deliberately, continue to invest energy in vectors contrary to our soul's needs and requirements, we soon experience a loss of energy, even depression such as I hit at mid-life. If we persist, the depression, the autonomous withdrawal of support from the soul, will only escalate in kind. Once again, the ego is invited to surrender its management system and shift priorities. Seldom do we enjoy this summons, for once again we are reminded that consciousness, with all its necessary gifts and accountabilities, is not really the boss after all.

And fifthly, most elusive of all, most important of all, is the question of meaning. We can live with much hardship, suffering, loss if we have a sense of purpose that is compelling. We can lose everything and still feel the deep support of the soul through the darkest hours if we know what we are doing provides us with meaning. In my darkest hours in Zürich— broke, broken, and alone—multiple voices in my head kept telling me to quit, yet I knew I was doing the only thing I could do to come out the other side. When my son Timothy died, I joined a club no one wishes to join, but I knew I best honored him by keeping his memory at the forefront of my life, and serving the values we had in common. As Jung said so succinctly, the smallest of things with meaning are always greater than the largest of things without meaning. I wish our besotted culture, driven to power, status, flashy things, could remember that. And when they can't, that is why there is so much unhappiness and emptiness in those who have it all.

There is an old Bob Dylan song in which he avers "you gotta serve somebody." I would modify that only slightly to: you have to serve something, but you may need to decide whether it is large or small, or whether it deserves your life's investment. As Martin Luther King added, you have to know what you would die for before you can really begin to live for something. If we do not serve something larger than our history, or our fears, then we will have no real second half of life. In the first half, we are called to legitimately serve the demands of family life, school, work and relationship expectations, and all of this is critical to gaining ego strength and creating a presence in the world. In the later years, whenever the question really comes to us, the focus shifts to "what wants to enter the world through me?" Many parts of my personality could have retired some time ago, but I still feel a larger call to write, teach, and attend the work of analysis in these years of diminishing sands in the hourglass. The passion is still there, the drive, the calling, and I am rewarded in serving it by a profound sense of purpose, and a humbling gratitude for the privilege of knowing and serving what I was born to do.

An in-depth therapy will raise many more questions than it will answer. And this is the beginning of wisdom. Sometimes knowing what to ask, and knowing what we don't know is the prerequisite for the next stage of our development. Sometimes these questions have a distinct locus in our outer lives. How do I improve this relationship, or move on? How do I recover my personal authority? How do I deal with reverses and losses? How do I grow in spirit as the body declines in its capacities? How do I discern what new task the soul brings to me at this stage of the journey? For me recently, the question was, how to I retain a sense of autonomy and freedom while having to submit to medical regimens with large side effects? How do I sustain a sense of agency with diminishing capacities? These questions and others face all of us if we are privileged to live long enough. My wife and I consider ourselves very private, very independent persons, and we still shudder when we think of what we will face when one of us passes. Rollo May used to observe that many folks so fear being on their own that they never find themselves at all. Sooner or later, surrounded by people or not, we are all alone.

One way of looking at all this is: answers get you clarity for the moment, but questions get you a journey in which you learn that yesterday's answers no longer are sufficient for the summons of the new day. Among the questions I have suggested folks to ask in their therapy are the following. Many I have mentioned before, and many may be obvious to the reader, but they aren't always that obvious when one is in the midst of the doo-doo, when the way forward is obscure, and where no matter what you do it will hurt something that matters to you. Only in those moments do we have the next stage of our individuation process forming for us. Simple problems will have binary answers—do this or do that! But real crossroads in our growth will never have easy options.

We all wish to remain behind, of course, resting easy enough in whatever security we have at the moment, but Eros courses forward, incessantly burning this candle to its nub. We ask ourselves: *where have I been here before*, when I look at a questionable choice, behavior, or familiar outcome. Because we build on our experience, we often impose on new hours the frame, understanding, and strategies of the old. *What did this hit in me* is another form of that question. Also, *does this choice, this path, enlarge me or diminish me?* We usually know the answer to that question, and then are tasked with living what we know to be true. *What really matters to me, now,* in this crossroad of my life? Am I hanging on to something out of fear, sentimentality? *What primal fears still have their hooks in me,* despite the adult I have become? This question too immediately brings an agenda to the surface, and a task which we can no longer ignore. *What do I need to let go of* if I am going to take the next step into my journey? *What is wishing to be honored* in this life now? Am I still looking for permission to live this life? Am I still afraid of being out there on my own? Am I passing up one more chance at stepping into the largeness of this journey? Is there ever to be a moment where we find ourselves moving from fear to wonder, from encapsulation by complexes to a freedom never known before?

These are some of the questions that rise in the course of a sustained depth therapy. There is a place for problem solving, for dealing with immediate crises, but there is also a place in our lives for finally addressing *why* we are here, in this world, in this hour, and in this context. If we do not address this now, do we really think it will cease gnawing somewhere deeply within? Do I think the soul wants me to live a small, fear-driven life forever? Do I really think I cannot know now what I now know? And what I now know, can it not be a summons today, and tomorrow, for me?

When in some fashion we have asked and addressed these and similar questions, then we will have entered into a depth of engagement which honors the soul. Then we will have listened and attended (*therapeuein*) to the soul (*psyche*). And yes, it is a psychotherapy you can practice at home.

CHAPTER NINE

Invisible Means of Support:
The Theogonies of Stephen Dunn

Pulitzer Prize-winning poet Stephen Dunn was one of the finest American poets over the last fifty years. The two of us had adjacent offices back in academia and were very close friends and confidants for forty-eight years. He passed away in July of 2021 on his 82nd birthday, but he has not disappeared from the hearts of those who loved him and admired his insights into modern life. This essay was written to appear in the Festschrift honoring him in 2015: The Room and The World: Essays in Honor of the Poet Stephen Dunn— edited by one of our finest students, Laura McCullough, and reprinted here with her kind permission.

It might be argued that the last time the Western world made sense, that is, had a *Weltbild* to which those of all stations might subscribe, was around 1320, the time of the publication of Dante's *La Comedia*. For that brief while, king and commoner alike could look in one direction and see the medieval castle with its claim of both spiritual and civil authority, and in the other direction see the medieval cathedral with its similar claim. Together they provided the psycho-spiritual benchmarks, the points of reference, the longitudes and latitudes which allow one to know where one stands in some larger, cosmic picture. Moreover, Dante's vision crystallized an implicate hierarchy of values: directing one toward certain choices, measuring their worth, and construing their enduring consequences.

But, by 1348-49, almost half of Europe perished in the Black Death; the veins of royal claim began their long slow hemorrhage, and the mercantile, bourgeois secular city emerged as an alternative future. With the erosion of those old hierarchies, and fixed values, where, then, does one now stand, and how are our choices to be made? The first true "moderns" may be seen by 1600 in the spiritual desolation of Macbeth and the neurotic anguish of Hamlet, for, as Ulysses in *Troilus and Cressida* has it, "Untune that string, and hark what discord follows."

Put most succinctly, the intellectual and emotional duty of literary, philosophical, and artistic *modernism* is to critique the received structures and dismantle their explicit hierarchy of values. And the project of *post-modernism*, from Beckett to Stephen Dunn, is to figure out how one is to live amid enormous spiritual ambiguity thereafter: How does one make choices, in service to what, and framed by what larger perspective, if any at all?

As the epigraph to one of his early poems, Stephen Dunn cites the bon mot of Oscar Levant that an atheist is "someone with no invisible means of support." While there are so many themes one may profitably explore in Dunn's considerable oeuvre—the anfractuosities of intimate relationship, the ghosts of family past, the vanities and banalities of daily life—tracking the wisps, the fading traces of the departed gods makes him post-modern, and causes me most to hold him in regard. His work over the decades lies at the heart of this post-modern dilemma where one is obliged to reside, as the title of one of his books describes, *Between Angels,* in this hour Heidegger described as lying between the gods who have fled and the gods who have not yet come. Since we are all denizens of this dismal day, what Dunn explores is worthy of our respectful consideration, for the persistent question remains: What happens to the soul now, whither its journey, and by what lights does it navigate the tenebrous currents of our time?

Other modern and post-modern poets embodied this spiritual dislocation through the fracturing of their metaphors. Accordingly, we no longer find natural analogs such as the beloved described as "a red, red rose" (Burns) but rather discordant, dis-located images: a "patient etherized on a table" (Eliot) or ourselves as "the eyelids of defeated caves" (Tate). Quite consciously, Dunn takes up the project proclaimed by C. Day-Lewis to "move then with new desires / for where we used to live and love / is no-man's land / and only ghosts can live between two fires."

From his first book to his most recent, a replicative Dunn assignment is the ambiguous task of living in a god-haunted, god-abandoned world. With every flight from this task, its implicate importance reasserts itself. As Kenneth Burke suggested of Yeats's line, "that dolphin-torn, that gong-tormented sea," something presciently echoes in our unconscious as "that devil-torn, that god-tormented sea." In his first book, *Looking for Holes in the Ceiling*, Dunn describes how his poem's protagonist drills a hole in the ceiling, answers silly questions about it, turns it into a joke, until

> Gradually, I forget about it
> only a spider now and then
> reminds me
> of what foresight I had
> though there have been no messages
> not even a pole,
> nor a fireman.

> ("A Poem for Atheists")

In this near-comic trope, a hole in a ceiling, one nonetheless witnesses the dismantled hierarchy, the severed link between metaphysical layers once provided by sacred scriptures, tribal myth and ritual, and ecclesiastic authority to the transcendent Other—"thems what lives upstairs," as it were. This theme is echoed not only in Beckett's two tramps waiting by the roadside in perpetuity, but as mentioned earlier in Pinter's *The Dumbwaiter* where two inept thugs await their instructions from "on high." Comically garbled, absurd demands descend upon them via sinister scribbled scraps of paper, ending in murderous denouement. Or one thinks of Yeats again, who announces that since his "ladder" is gone, he is left only with the resources of "the foul rag and bone shop of the heart."

The Dantesque hierarchy, Jacob's ladder, Yggdrasil's spinning world-tree, the sacred mountain, the totem pole, the central axis of tent or tabernacle, the smaragdine tablets of Hermes Trismegisthus—all vanished! When the vertical is gone, only the horizontal plane remains, though echoes linger: "My voice still reflects the time / I believed in prayer as a way of getting / what I wanted." ("Biography in the First Person") And, we go in search of some fine simulacrum spirit: "dig up the brandy / you buried the year before. / Taste it. It will taste like / the musk of a religion / you gave up / for the sweeter taste of women." ("Chipping Away at Death") In these last lines one sees two perennial but pallid surrogates for the gods: booze, sex, and many other seductions of soul.

An elemental psycho-spiritual fact, or better, psycho-dynamic, is that when "the gods" are not experienced as felt presences, we will project our need for them onto objects of desire. The generalized answer to the spiritual aridity of modernism has been either the infantilizing regression of fundamentalism or the distractions of popular culture.

Neither is new. In the seventeenth century, mystic and mathematician Blaise Pascal noted that his contemporary popular culture was a vast *divertissement*, or diversion, lest anyone stumble into the magnitude of their emptied souls. Or, as Jung put it in a letter, the "modern" fell off the roof of the medieval cathedral into the abyss of the unconscious. When the gods are lost, the concomitant vacuum experienced generates disorders of desire; hence, narcotics of various stripe and materialism serve as our chief treatment plans for this existential dilemma. If either anodyne worked, we would know it by now. The dirty little secret of our time is that we all <u>do</u> know it, and pretend that we do not. I once had a client who incessantly bought automobiles, several a year. A child of poverty and a harsh domestic life, he projected the numinous onto those shiny pieces of metal that cruised by his emotionally sterile home. To him they were freedom, mobility, and most of all, emotional connection. While he laughed at his own automobile obsession, a failed fetish to an unknown god, he could not shake their hold on his psyche, a measure of how deep the need for connection with the transcendent Other runs in us. All addictions, all disorders of desire are, in Rimbaud's memorable phrase, *Une Saison d'Enfer*, a season in Hell, mostly because it is a hell we cannot help but keep choosing.

So what, then, is the alternative? How does one accept one's estrangement, live in this world, and manage to make any sense of it? So much of Dunn's work has been precisely to address this dilemma, and yet is clear that his answers are his alone, and not meant as recommendations to the rest of us. He despises prophets, pedagogues, demagogues, preachers, and politicians. As for his own alienation, he readily confesses that he carries metaphors dangerously close to complacency concealed in the heel of his shoe ("On

Hearing the Airlines Will Use a Psychological Profile to Catch Potential Skyjackers") yet when "they wanted me to tell the truth, / I said I lived among them / for years, a spy, / but all that I wanted was love." ("What They Wanted"). Most of all Dunn finds his personal path in the precincts of love—the love of friends, of a good drink, of a fall-away jumper that swishes the net, in the absurdity of the pompous, in irony, perversity, surprises and reversals, and most of all, this most spiritual of men confesses, "I love the corporeal body itself, / designed to fail, / and the mind, the helpless mind, / so often impelled to think about it." Next to, perhaps, Yeats's summary that "man is in love, and loves what vanishes. / What more is there to say?" could we find a more succinct definition of our common condition? Granted the dual gift of life, and the consciousness of its precious transience, we owe two things: a life fully lived, and a life relinquished finally. In the meantime, there is the living to do, with only the shabby tools, the inadequate instruments provided us. We remain, "designed to fail," but impelled to ruminate on its perplexities. Again, Yeats reminds us that out of the quarrel with others rhetoric rises, and out of the quarrel with ourselves the possibility of poetry, or perhaps an honest psychology. Designed to fail, and yet impelled to ruminate— what better definition of the split we carry, the neurosis we serve? From such ruin only creativity rises to soften and ennoble our suffering, and thereby move us from the merely pathetic to the occasionally tragic.

R. M. Rilke suggested that the vocation of the poet was, at heart, to praise—to praise what is, to praise the wonder and terror of it all. In *Between Angels*, Dunn depicts a metaphoric guardian angel who might also be seen as both the persona and ministry of the poet himself,

...in for the long haul, trying to live

beyond despair, he believes, he needs
to believe
everything he does takes root, hums

beneath the surfaces of the world.

This hope is not hubris; it is the genuine contribution of the creative soul to our fragmented world, a world in which poetry, as Edna St. Vincent Millay noted, does not build the bridge nor mend the broken bone, but may still feed the soul—and the deprivation of which causes us all to sicken and to die long before we are dead. Rilke spoke of the poet as "a bee of the Invisible," Ezra Pound described the poet as "the antennae of the human race," and for Dunn this hum he hears and tracks is the sound of *Dasein*,["Being-itself," *Sein* + "thrown there," *da*.] thrust into this world, humming within our veins, the same resonant energies which move the stars, and once constellated the myths of our ancestors.

Dunn's "myth" for a myth-impoverished time is that we are between angels now, and their ancient task falls, absurdly, to us.

Between angels, on this earth
absurdly between angels, I
try to navigate

in the bluesy middle ground...
("Between Angels")

Whatever the old forms the gods incarnated, when one of Them appears to Dunn in "Dancing with God," he is attired rather shabbily this time, still mysterious, still perplexing, and still always leaving: "He left then, no thanks, / no sign / that he'd felt anything / more than an earthly moment...." ("Dancing with God"). But the speaker remains, confused, puzzled, fully aware of being, as Yeats put it, "sick with desire and fastened to a dying animal."

Dunn accepts the absurdity of this present moment in which we are vested. When Camus observed that life was meaningful precisely because it is absurd, I take it that he argues that any "meaning" presented to us is someone else's package, and not necessarily ours. Ours is rather to be pieced together through our existential revolt, in our hopeless, extinction-bound but luminous pause between the great mysteries. Both Camus and Dunn turned to Sisyphus as the prototype of this paradox. When he *chooses* to roll the fated boulder up the fated hill to fall back in its fated way, he wrests from the gods their terrible autonomy and with it a measure of spiritual freedom. At such a moment, Dunn imagines,

> The gods sank back
> in their airy chairs, Sisyphus sensed
> he had taken something from them,
> more on his own than ever now.
>   ("Sisyphus's Acceptance")

As an artist, amid this Sisyphean mélange we call our lives, Dunn proffers a final wish for us:

> I've tried
> to clear a late-century place for us
> in among the shards. Lie down,
> tell me what you need.
> Here is where loveliness can live

with failure, and nothing's complete,
I love how we go on.
("Loves")

So, we are *here*, for *now*, and then we are *not* here...and in the meantime, we go on. In *Walking Light: Essays and Memoirs*, Dunn approvingly quotes fellow poet Stanley Kunitz, "I dream of an art so transparent that you can look through and see the world."

This is Dunn's achievement: a lens through which we see ourselves, in which the absurdities and opacities of our moment are briefly illumined, and in which—through the connective tendrils of art—we resonate with what hums beneath the surface. Dunn's poems are a tacit petition to mystery, and a deep confession that even we may, from time to time, experience invisible means of support.

CHAPTER TEN

The Resources Within Each of Us

"The moment is not properly an atom of time, but an atom of eternity."

Søren Kierkegaard

Being a reminder that we are equipped by nature, or Divinity, with the inherent resources to not only survive but take more and more ownership of our lives that we might add our small chip to the great mosaic of being.

We carry within an *entelechy*, a goal, an end (*telos*) to which our psyche aspires. As we all learned, and rather early, such a summons, and challenge, is of course overwhelmed early by the circumstances of life. Of all the traumata that afflict us, no doubt the most damaging is the loss of this connection to the source within. Only in moments when alone, or in dreams which come to us, do we sometimes recapture a flickering moment of that primordial connection. Over two centuries ago, Wordsworth must have had an intuitive opening into vertical time (*kairos*, the transcendence of linear time into a realm of timelessness versus the slow tick of day after day, breath after breath of *chronos* time). That momentary aperture into his childhood called him back to what once was, but is no longer. Amid the beauty of the Lake District in North-Western England, in the lengthy poem *The Prelude* he writes:

> When from our better selves we have too long
> Been parted by the hurrying world, and droop,
> Sick of its business, of its pleasures tired,
> How gracious, how benign is Solitude!

Later in that same century his countryman Matthew Arnold similarly intuited the presence of some "other" within.

> In a poem titled "The Buried Life," he reflects:

> ...often, in the world's most crowded streets,
> often, in the din of strife,
> There rises an unspeakable desire
> After the knowledge of our buried life;
> A thirst to spend our fire and restless force
> In tracking out our true, original course;
> A longing to inquire
> Into the mystery of this heart which beats
> So wild, so deep in us—to know
> Whence our lives come and where they go.

And later still, modern American poet William Stafford concludes in a poem, "The Way It Is,"

> There's a thread you follow. It goes among
> things that change. But it doesn't change.

168

People wonder about what you are pursuing.
You have to explain about the thread.[21]

He adds that as long as we hold to that thread we can't get lost. All the good and terrible stuff happens as it will happen, and nothing we do will spare us suffering and extinction, but, he admonishes us, "You don't ever let go of the thread."

What is central to these examples is clear, that there is something within each of us, some presence, some intelligence, some wisdom that transcends the limitations of our ego. Jung goes a step further and personifies this other when he writes,

> "in each of us there is another whom we do not know. He speaks to us in dreams, and tells us how differently he sees us from the way we see ourselves. When, therefore, we find ourselves in a difficult situation to which there is no solution, he can sometimes kindle a light that radically alters our attitude—the very attitude that led us into the difficult situation."[22]

The legacy of childhood is such that we all feel overwhelmed by the prospects of living fully, managing all that comes at us, and naturally we look to others for clues, for support. I mentioned earlier how much I depended on books to learn how to be a proto-adult, and how hungrily I sought clues for managing fear, conflict, and doubt. Only later in life would

---

[21] https://wordsfortheyear.com/2017/10/19/the-way-it-is-by-william-stafford/

[22] Jung, "The Meaning of Psychology for Modern Man," *CW 10, Civilization in Transition*, para. 325.

I learn that those emotional states were normal, and not inherently pathological. Since no one else was letting on, or telling me otherwise, I assumed that there was something terribly flawed in me. And most of my patients, from childhood to the present, have so assumed as well. That is why I wrote *Swamplands of the Soul* to "normalize" what felt so abnormal, and to depathologize pathology.

Jung reminds us that "The psyche is not of today; its ancestry goes back many millions of years. Individual consciousness is only the flower and the fruit of a season, sprung from the perennial rhizome beneath the earth; and it would find itself in better accord with the truth if it took the existence of the rhizome into its calculations." [23] This timeless zone, this archetypal field of energy is the inheritance of all of us. Our ancestors treasured and preserved the stories that linked them to such generative heritages. Foundation myths of ancient lands informed their flock of this profound trans-personal origin, and the sustaining continuity they carried within them. Our sensation-driven, speed-besotted time has severed that link. We think ourselves simply self-made critters, and reside mostly in the realm of ego-driven agendas. Such is a grand delusion, and like any belief, it owns us until we can stand outside it, and ask: "How well is this working for me, really?" (A former client from A. A. reported the aphorism in his meeting that perhaps applies to us all, "This isn't working for me, but I do it very well.")

One doesn't have to go very far within to reach the primitive regions of our species, our untamed feral selves. There we are just as capable of "possession" as our ancestors were by forces they knew not. Because consciousness is so permeable, whatever floods up from below becomes our operating fiction for the moment. Only when we can step

---

[23] Jung, *CW5, Symbols of Transformation*, p. xxiv.

outside ourselves can we begin to recover a purchase on this radical moment in this world in this hour.

You may recall being utterly transported by "love," and utterly devastated by its loss. Little did you know that you were caught up in a limerence—a projection of your self-sufficient system under the spell of a complex that denigrated your capacities—that informed you that you were incapable of living a full life without the necessary "other." How many bereft souls have taken their lives, believing they cannot exist without that necessary buttressing of the other for their shaky selves? When you were a sophomore in high school, such limerence moments probably happened at least once per semester. And for some, it is much more recent than that.

Generally speaking, the chief agenda of the ego is to obtain as much security as possible, gain sovereignty over the external world to the degree it can, and quell the disturbances which rise from within as much as possible. In practice, we all find the psyche thwarting that ordering agenda, bringing us the same old same old, or confounding us by undoing plans, proposals, projects, and prognostications. In those moments of befuddlement to the ego, we naturally look to find someone to blame. If no one is convenient, we can then blame ourselves, and the shames, guilts, and recriminations take over their familiar persecutory roles. This is why Jung commented that what we deny inwardly will tend to come to us in the outer world though we will likely assign the blame to fate, or the acts of others. His reminder is really scary, at least to me, but it also can slap us upside the head, get the ego to pay attention, and realize that only what we can set right in ourselves can we have a hope of setting right in the world.

It is precisely that thwarting of the will that can also bring us to a reconsideration of our relationship to what is unknown within us. However, it usually takes a significant amount of frustration before we begin to look within. As I mentioned in my life, I had achieved all that I was supposed to do with my life, as my consciousness believed at the time, and only when the psyche stoutly refused cooperation did I begin to question anything. Most folks, sooner or later, have to ask the question: What is going on here? What do I need to attend? Where is this coming from in me, or some question like that. Only then does the pose and posture of the ego begin to soften.

While ego wishes to remove the discomfort through a magic pill, a set of proactive steps, a thirty-day program, the fact is, none of those things work in any lasting way. Jung makes this process much more problematic and asks us to completely revision the conflicts, symptoms, and suffering that often comes to us:

> We should not try to 'get rid' of a neurosis but rather to experience what it means, what it has to to teach, what its purpose is. We should even learn to be thankful for it, otherwise we pass it by and miss the opportunity of getting to know ourselves as we really are. A neurosis is truly removed only when it has removed the false attitude of the ego. We do not cure it—it cures us.[24]

This is a stunning reframing of our usual ego position. We wish sovereignty in our lives, control, and yet something else has taken over instead. How could we ever be grateful for this overthrow? Even in his memoir, *Memories, Dreams, Reflections*, Jung repeatedly says that here is another thing

---

[24] Jung, *CW 10, Civilization in Transition*, "The State of Psychotherapy Today," para. 361.

he didn't know about himself, and it felt like a defeat. How is it a defeat when this revolt is engineered by the psyche (soul), unless it is the ego that is whining over its superseded phantasies once again?

Sooner or later, the ego state, as we have seen, has to submit to something. If it does not submit to a larger story, a more challenging and empowering narrative, it is submitting to something derivative, demeaning, and ultimately, diminishing.

In writing about "The Aims of Psychotherapy" in 1929, Jung observed that the therapeutic project is less about "cure," for life is not a disease, but an on-going experiment to be lived through. So, the common work, he asserts, "is less a question of treatment than of developing the creative possibilities latent within the patient."[25]

As projects of nature, we are infinitely adaptable, resilient, and resourceful. Without these attributes, this animal species we are would not have been able to survive the perils of this planet. Just as we adapt to the various powers around us, adaptations that often distort, even violate our own souls, so we manage to wedge ourselves into the narrow slots where external forces so often maneuver us. While these adaptations allow us to fit into our family structures, or social environments, they also tend to cost us a great deal. Every adaptation, however obliged by outer pressures, risks a further injury to the psyche which will not go unaddressed by the soul. So, bombarded as we are by the cacophonous claims of contemporary culture, we find ways to fit in; and the hidden cost of doing so shows up in our disturbing dreams, our anaesthetizing addictions, or our

---

[25] Jung, *CW 16, The Practice of Psychotherapy*, "The Aims of Psychotherapy," para. 82.

sundry forms of denial or distraction. How many of us, for example, have tried to do "the right thing," as defined by our family messages, our cultural imperatives and prohibitions, or by succumbing to the pressures of the hour, and then felt empty within, used, exploited, betrayed somehow? The perverse irony is that these same adaptations that often allow us to "fit in," become traps, constraints which also contain or deform the developmental desires that course through us as well.

Only when we understand psychopathology as the quite legitimate protest of the psyche, a summons to take seriously a wider range of life's choices, do we realize that we do have an internal guidance system. If I am doing all "the right things," why is it I have to keep forcing the energy, fighting off the doubts, depressions, and keep trying to stay ahead of whatever is pursuing me?

Jung speaks to this common phenomenon quite clearly and powerfully. He notes that so many of his cases "are not suffering from any clinically definable neurosis, but from the senselessness and aimlessness of their lives. I should not object if this were called the general neurosis of our age."[26]

Most of us really "know" what is right for us, though we may be frightened or intimidated to know what we already know. As Jung put it, "Most of my patients knew the deeper truth, but did not live it. And why did they not live it? Because of that bias which makes us all live from the ego, a bias which comes from overvaluation of the conscious mind."[27] And by "conscious mind," generally Jung means the mind that is so frequently occupied by the complex triggered in that moment. So, seldom are we "in our right mind." Most of the

---

[26] Ibid., para. 83.
[27] Ibid., para. 108.

time we are subsumed by, and serving, the invisible text of a "message," which means we serve the received authority rather than our own deepest promptings.

So much of the deceptive self-help genre prattles on about "happiness." "Thirty Days to this or That..." "Five Easy Steps to..." You fill in the blanks. But this pablum does not feed the soul, fire the spirit, create the new world. The pursuit of "happiness" is delusory. It is a by-product of those rare moments of détente, of concordance between our external choices and our internal reality. As he writes in another essay, "Psychotherapy and a Philosophy of Life," "The principle aim of psychotherapy is not to transport the patient to an impossible state of happiness but to help him acquire steadfastness and philosophic patience in the face of suffering. Life demands for its completion and fulfilment a balance between joy and sorrow."[28]

In the end, we prove to be more than just social animals; we are meaning-seeking, meaning-creating creatures. As Jung notes, "The least of things with a meaning is always worth more in life than the greatest of things without it."[29]

When we reflect a moment, it is the natural desire and tendency of conscious life to solve problems and then move on. This proclivity does indeed lead to the resolution of many if not most of life's dilemmas. But not the ones that matter most. Jung himself shared our desire to quick and happy resolution to the conflicts and stuck places. He describes, "I had always worked with the temperamental conviction that at bottom there are no insoluble problems, and experience justified me in so far as I have often seen patients simply outgrow a problem that had destroyed

---

[28] Ibid., para. 185.
[29] Ibid., para. 45.

others. This 'outgrowing,' as I formerly called it, proves on further investigation to be a new level of consciousness. Some higher or wider interest appeared on the patient's horizon, and through this broadening of outlook the insoluble problem lost its urgency. It is not solved logically in its own terms, but faded out when confronted with a new and stronger life urge."[30]

How often the old adage "sleep on it" does bring a measure of relief the next day when we have been able to step back out of the emotional morass and reframe it in some way. Our unconscious has also worked on it to provide a new perspective. Many notable artistic and scientific discoveries have also risen out of this outer/inner world dialectic.

Still, many of life's issues are not solvable. For example, sometimes quanta of trauma remain in our system and send up bubbles to trouble our days, just as a sunken ocean liner releases its flotsam for decades. Sometimes betrayals, profound losses, roads not taken continue to haunt a person and cloud the present. We will never "solve" these experiences for they are always part of our psychoactive history. But consciously we can attend to the business of living in the present. Asking the question, "What does this old, persisting problem make me do, or keep me from doing," obliges us to take responsibility for what spills into the world through us. It also tends to pull us out of the disabling past into an engaging, demanding present.

Elsewhere, Jung writes eloquently about those dilemmas to which there is no obvious resolution, or no cost-free resolution. Then he suggests we hold the tension of opposites which are pulling us apart, until the "third" appears. The "third" means, neither this nor that, yes or no,

---

[30] Jung, CW 13, *Alchemical Studies*, "Commentary on the Secret of the Golden Flower," para. 17.

but what is the developmental task this dilemma brings me? Where am I being asked to grow larger than either option, to reframe, to reposition this contretemps? In asking this question, once again, we are moved from a paralysis, a stuckness, a loss of agency to a summons to accountability. And as we are all driven to admit, being accountable is what it means to be a grown-up.

For those of us who may, from time to time, feel utterly defeated by some contretemps, some recalcitrant dilemma, and blame ourselves, the Gods, or each other, Jung summarizes, "The greatest and most important problems of life are fundamentally insoluble. They must be so, for they express the necessary polarity inherent in every self-regulating system. They can never be solved, but only outgrown."[31] Meanwhile, the task of living goes onward, with or without our conscious participation.

Often we may catch ourselves envying others, thinking they have an easier life, or possess some magic we have not yet found. But all envy of others is predicated on the perception that someone else has what I want, or need. In fact, four of the so-called seven deadly sins are in service to the unconscious conclusion that "I am not enough in myself, and thus I must possess that other somehow"—they are greed, lust, envy, and gluttony. In particular, envy is a failure to remember that we are all made of the same cosmic dust, the same soul-stuff, coursing toward the same leveling end, and as carriers of the life force into the next aeon, we are presently provided within all that is needed to survive and prevail.

Yes, it is true, life is fringed with the seven D's: defeat, decline, drift, desuetude, depression, despair, death.

---

[31] Ibid., para. 18.

Why bother with anything at all, when all our noisy circuses are ringed with death? That is the voice of the Tempter—whether whispering from without or from within us—the one who whispers life is too hard, that the struggle is futile, and there is nothing still to be discovered about ourselves, about each other, and about the great mystery in which we swim. Still, this summons to discovery goes on till our last breath, and stops only when we fail to be curious, to wonder, or to explore.

As Thomas Merton summarized it, "What can we gain by sailing to the moon if we are not able to cross the abyss that separates us from ourselves? This is the most important of all voyages of discovery, and without, all the rest are not only useless, but disastrous." We begin to cross that abyss that separates within when we learn to trust our deepest feelings, our energy systems, our dreams, and all the natural promptings that rise from our animal compass, not different from that which orients other animals to live their inwardly directed life. The addition of the summons to meaning is what both characterizes this animal and differentiates it. This animal can actually sacrifice its life on behalf of an abstraction, a cause, a flag, an ideology. This animal suffers disconnect from meaning, and though we all patch things over as best we can, something within continues to reach up to us, touch us, and recall us to our journey.

Writing over a century ago, Jung describes our time so well. "Today there are countless neurotics who are neurotic simply because they cannot be happy in their own way— they do not even know that the fault lies with them."[32] He goes on to say, such "normal" people are adrift because they too have no compelling symbol to direct libido or psychic

---

[32] Jung, *CW5*, *Symbols of Transformation*, para. 342.

energy in a developmental way. They have no larger story that provides a narrative structuring toward a timeless locus, a longitude and latitude for their soul.

The erosion of mythic systems that once connected ancestors to the four orders of meaning—cosmos, nature, tribe, and selfhood—have left so many with seductive but spiritually impoverished and deceptive images such as a new car, a shiny phone, a soporific drug, or complex-driven ideology. And yet, restorative and directive symbols arise from our dreams, and from our soul's ferment. If ever we can learn to trust what rises from within, dialogue with it, and honor it, we will approach the precincts of the old gods again. While we may not employ their depleted names, we may gain renewed access to their energies, and enter life again in a new and deeper way.

CHAPTER ELEVEN

Notes Toward a Personal Memoir

You, sent out beyond your recall,
go to the limits of your longing.
                                                    R M Rilke

Being a personal offering to mirror to the reader why, and how, the exploration of formative memories in our lives is much more than nostalgia, but rather is a summons to an enlarged awareness of what drives us still, undermines us, and may well bring to the surface what unfinished business remains.

I never plan to write a memoir or an autobiography, hence the key word *toward* above. So this essay is rather a processing of memories that keep coming to the surface, apparently because there is some serious affect attached. I do not write this to be self-indulgent or waste the reader's time. Each of these memories will, I hope, stir some issue worth examining. I have found so many folks over sixty-five having such memories come to the surface, or they appear in their dreams, unbidden by consciousness. I do not think this is the fabled nostalgia whereby "seniors" are charged with "living in the past." Rather, I think it is how the psyche continues to work on what happened, how it affects us, what it perhaps made us do or blocked us from doing, as well as querying how did we understand it then, and how do we understand it now? Occasionally, this process also brings up unfinished business.

So, the psyche is not idling; it is continuing its mythmaking process, and paying attention only deepens the understanding and the mystery of our journey on this earth. In his current book, *Four Thousand Weeks*, my friend Oliver Burkeman reminds us that if we are privileged to live to eighty, as I have, that is all we get. It is a pathetically short time, especially since we are conscious of sands ticking through the proverbial hourglass. (The history of what we recognize as humankind has only been on this planet a little over 300,000 weeks.) So, here are a few recollections, a few reverberations, a few perseverations.

I was born in 1940 in Springfield, Illinois in Lincoln's hometown and tomb while the depression was still dominating America. Much of the rest of the world was already in a death struggle. Japan had invaded China three years before, producing such cultural wonders as the Rape of Nanking, and Hitler had laid most of Poland waste, and was already setting up concentration camps, while England and France were hanging on by their fingernails. When I was born, the Wehrmacht was squeezing the British Expeditionary Force toward a town called Dunquerque. As distant as my family was from these horrors, I soon knew my parents were affected by them, and by the extreme economic hardship that affected daily life. While I was safe, the world was not, and I absorbed the general atmosphere that blanketed this country and the world.

When Pearl Harbor brought us into the conflagration, my father and his younger brother, Dale, went to enlist in the army. My dad was considered too old by then; he had a family, and he was already in a vital industry. Namely, he worked for the Allis-Chalmers Company that built tractors and graders and soon would be building tanks. But Dale was accepted, and he went off to the South Pacific where he was in combat in New Guinea and the Philippines. He left with coal-black hair, in his 20's, and came home in the fall of 1945 with his hair totally white. During those early years as we walked through the neighborhood, there were pennons hanging in the front windows with stars on them, indicating a son was in the military. Some of them were gold indicating he wasn't coming home. Dad was sent to Racine, Wisconsin to liaison with the tank-building industry there and came in on the train every two weeks. He always hid some small token or toy in his suitcase, so I was eager to see not only him but what I could find amid the clothing. We lived with severe rationing then and finding an orange, or a banana, or my favorite, fig bars, was a big moment. I also overheard things that children are not to hear. For example, one day I heard them whisper that under the stamp of a postcard from a P.O.W. had said in code, "They cut my tongue out." Whether that was wartime atrocity rumor or not, much worse than that is now well documented. Needless to say, the child thought about that prospect during the nighttime hours. I grew used to going to the train station to see the soldiers and my father climb aboard and disappear in the noise and smoke. There was much weeping at those stations.

In late 1945 when I was over five, Uncle Dale came back. Out of touch for many months before, he came to our house in the middle of the night because Grandfather was suffering a severe heart condition, and he didn't want to shock him by just walking in on him. I remember that night just as clearly as if it were last week. My parents woke me to meet my Uncle Dale whom I didn't remember from the time he went to war. My mother said to him, "I am so glad the war is finally over." He said, "Yes, but they say it's just going to continue and move elsewhere." "Where, who," she replied? Dale said, "They say it is now going to be with Russia." My Mother replied, "What does their flag look like?" "It's red with a hammer and a sickle." I knew what a hammer was, but I asked, "What is a sickle?" They explained. What is so astonishing to me is that the average soldier, in the fall of 1945 already knew we were in a soon-to-be-called Cold War with the Stalinist Soviet state.

The point of my memory is not to recall an interesting tidbit but to reflect on a contemporaneous atmosphere which affected me then and abides with me still. I grew immensely aware of a world of conflict, suffering, and heartache. In fact, as a child, I believed I was destined for what I call the *Three W's*: work, war, and worry. They have traveled with me all along the way. When I was approximately between four and seven years old, I used to go and sing aloud on a street corner, to no one but myself and the universe, songs popular at the time: *"Now is the Hour"* (when we must say goodbye), *"(There'll Be Bluebirds Over) The White Cliffs of Dover,"* and *"We'll Meet Again" (don't know where, don't know when).* All of them were songs of separation, loss, and hope for better times. They embody what in the Renaissance was called *compathia*, "shared suffering."

I think my singing those songs was my solidarity with the world's woe. I was safe, but my integument was very permeable, and I keenly felt the suffering around me. All of that has stayed with me, and colored my entire life, and I wasn't even in danger as so many other, less fortunate children obviously were. I think it gave me a somewhat melancholic perspective on the world, which I've tried to "treat" through humor, athletics, and learning as much about it all as I could. A local librarian, my local "pusher," recognized a reader in me and allowed me the run of the library, and so I came home with all books on the war I could hold. One of the first books I recall reading was not "See Dick Run, See Jane Run" but a book on the bloody fighting at Guadalcanal in the Solomons. In fact, I don't remember reading any children's books after age six or seven.

It is no surprise to folks in the helping professions to learn that contemporaneous atmospheres, ranging from the dynamics of home life to the field of international conflicts, affect a person's worldview and values. As an example, recall the account by Stephen Dunn cited earlier in this work about the unspoken elephant in the room which governed his parent's relationship, and around which the child had to silently orbit. Accordingly, from childhood on, I have always had a voice in my head, even in the best times, that reminds me, "Yes, but recall just down the street, people are going through painful hours, or are getting hurt in some terrible way." It didn't make me depressed, or morose, or dysphoric, but amid the many sunny days and a truly hopeful disposition, it was always sobering and balanced my view of life. That other cheerful soul, Samuel Beckett, reminds us that the quantity of tears in the world is always a constant. Where someone is laughing, someone elsewhere must be weeping. There are those who would think this attitude is neurotic; I think it is realistic, caring, and balanced. That voice from childhood travels with me into this ninth decade, and keeps me mindful of the great cosmic scale in which we are all balanced—neither too high nor too low. Or, as I frequently say, life is serious, for real, may sooner or later break your heart, and oh, yes..."have a nice day, y'all!"

* * *

My grandmother, Edna Lindgren, lost her husband, a Swedish immigrant coal miner, to a cave in. There were no insurances, no pensions, no handshakes even, and so she survived on sewing, a skill which she had mastered. I could tell that she was very bright and curious but had never had the opportunity of an education. When I was very young and she asked what I was interested in, I replied, among things I forget now, "history." "Modern or ancient history," she pursued. I thought a moment and concluded, "Well, all history is ancient to me, and so I said 'ancient.'" The next birthday brought me a book on Greece and Rome, and I was most struck by a photo of a painting therein. It depicted Roman mothers sending their sons off to a foreign war in chariots and phalanx formation. I had seen such formations in my own time, with a tank or two thrown in. But underneath the painting was this admonition from the mothers to their sons, "Come back victorious, or come back on your shields." Ooh, those mothers were serious I thought, and it certainly reinforced a child's notion that as a boy I was expected to fulfil such a summons as well.

Also, during this time, we went walking in a nearby park where we happened to run into three soldiers from the Chinese Nationalist army. What they were doing in the middle of the Midwest, we had no idea whatsoever.[33] But my grandmother was a friendly soul, and we sat down and talked with them. They spoke English poorly, but we could understand them, and even I grasped that they were terribly homesick for their troubled homeland. (The Japanese army

---

[33] Research later informed me that many Chinese were sent to the Midwest to form a new army to return to China to fight the invading Chinese. At least I confirmed that I had not hallucinated.

had really whipped the Chinese army but for the arrival of British, Indian, and American help. Their greater foe, Mao's mob, was shortly headed toward them like being down river when the Yangtze is at flood stage.) My grandmother invited them to lunch at her home, and we five walked there together. They seemed taken by this American child, perhaps seeing themselves as lost children, and were very affectionate to me. They pulled out their coins from their pockets and gave them to me. I had never seen a coin with a hole in it before. I was touched by their gifts and swore to keep them always. To this day, I regret having lost them in the decades and moves to follow. After the war, my grandmother received a letter from one of them, which told us they had returned to the safety of mainland China and thanking us. I never forgot them, and always wondered how long they got to live after that for they were still soldiers in Chang Kai-Shek's army. Again, all this reinforced my melancholic sense of the painful separations, losses, and great sorrow that war brings to this world.

* * *

Living in Springfield, our nearest repository of history was easily found in the large imprint the Great Rail-splitter left on his home city. Not only was his home two miles away, but his tomb also, the state house for Illinois then, and his corner law office as well. And New Salem, where Lincoln became an adult and first fell in love, and lost Anne Rutledge to the fevers, was only 24 miles away. I implored my parents to take me there at least one time per year. (Later in high school, one of my classmates named Herndon was a direct descendent of William Herndon, Lincoln's law partner.) History that real was very rich and always fired my imagination. Each year 4th of July, a state representative, and later a federal representative in the Eisenhower era named G. William Horsley, (1910-96) whose physique was lanky and who wore a beard, stood on the steps of Lincoln's home and stentoriously recited the Gettysburg Address. One year my grandmother and I left early and walked to 8th and Jackson and arrived before anyone else. I stood there the whole time (the speech is short you remember), rapt, hands wrapped around my back, and wholly attentive. To my surprise the next morning, there Grandmother and I were on the front page of the then *Illinois State Journal*. I took so seriously Lincoln's words and values, and still do, and still hurt to see them so seldom emulated. Having Lincoln as a personal hero figure, and Lou Gehrig also, was quite appropriate for a child for they both modeled a person who came from nothing, and who through dint of effort and discipline, entered into a larger life. Both had traumatic endings, cut off before their time, and both remained as templates throughout my life. It's not that I expected any public acclaim, but I wanted to try to be something like the kind of person they seemed to be— quiet, serious, and conscientious. There are worse models for a boy, or for an adult.

* * *

Like other boys I occasionally got into trouble, and like other boys did things of which I was ashamed. One I will tell you. All boys then had Daisy BB guns, air rifles that shot a tiny pellet perhaps 200 feet or so. Once, sitting in my grandmother's tree, I heard a bird singing in a neighbor's tree. I could hear it but not see it. Without grasping the implications of my act, I closed my eyes, put the rifle in a crook of a branch, and going by sound alone tried to imagine where to point the muzzle. I shot, the singing stopped, and a feather flew out of the distant tree and fluttered to the ground. I went over the fence, and there it was dead. I was astonished that by sound alone I aimed that weapon. And I felt instantly ashamed of what I had done. That was my Ancient Mariner albatross. I had killed something "gratuitously." For no reason other than to do it. A thoughtless boy, a thoughtless act, and I never forgot it. After reading Dostoevsky's 1863 *Notes from Underground* wherein he debunks Plato's conviction that a human would only do evil out of ignorance, and argues rather that sometimes a person simply does things gratuitously, for no reason, and with nary a rationalization. I guess I was ignorant then, but I also knew I was responsible.

That moment led me to a troubling question then: if I was to be a soldier, how could I ever shoot another human being. Much later, I read the research of soldier and historian S. L. A. Marshall that revealed that in multiple wars, even in those units directly engaged in combat against an enemy, fewer than 25% actually fired their weapons. This statistic is stunning, but other studies seemed to support its conclusions, suggesting, as Marshall also argued, that deep inside men do not want to kill other men. After that I did not want to kill anything. When I later had a shotgun, I used it only for target practices against inanimate objects. While we come from a culture that has been violent and predatory since its arrival on these shores, a culture that worships violence, I suspect my experience is found in the souls of most other men, even those who did shoot their weapons. I never judge them for that for I knew I also had it in my own heart and soul.

And, like other boys, I used to take chances that would have turned my cautious and protective parents to stone if they knew. My grade school friend, Luke Haag, later to become a national ballistics expert, and I decided that the creek nearby must flow into the Sangamon River that must flow into the Illinois River that must flow into the mighty Mississippi that must flow, like the Illinois Central also that blew through town, all the way down to Noo Awleens. So, we began borrowing...uh... pilfering pieces of wood and large lard cans and slowly, quietly built us a raft. We finally finished it, packed our bags with food, and prepared to launch. The damn thing was impossibly heavy, but we worked our tails off dragging it through brush to creek's edge. Finally, we slid it into the water and set sail, Captain Courageous and Sinbad the Sailor. We got less than 100 yards before the mighty craft wedged on a sandbar and was hopelessly stuck. We left it there and never told anyone about this shameful failure. That was, after all, benign. That same Luke and I did engage in more reprehensible moments thereafter.

There was a high railroad trestle that was probably 50 feet or so off the ground, a lethal height. So, we scaled that private property, climbed on top of the tracks and set off merrily on our marvelous adventure. About half way across, suddenly we heard a train whistle and a train bearing down on us. We couldn't make it to either end of the trestle and we couldn't jump. It was one of those decisive moments Søren Kierkegaard described where the event is launched, and there is no going back. We had only one choice and that was to hang by our hands on the trestle and dangle there while the train roared over us. If you have ever had a train roll over you, you know what a tremendous roar that is. It shakes one to the bones. Afterwards, we fled, assuming the engineer would call the police on us, and also so traumatized by the event that we were speechless. I think it was an instant, silent compact between us never to tell anyone about that incident, knowing it might filter back to our parents. To this day, I think of that poor engineer and his trauma, thinking he was about to kill two boys as he couldn't stop in time. I would apologize if I could. And I am still wondering if anyone will tell the police and this will finally get back to our long-deceased parents. Still, I am glad we did it.

* * *

There were two intimations of the future for me, a future that would lead me away from Springfield. In my childhood there were very few airplanes. When I heard one, I would run outside and follow it as far as I could. When I was a child, there were still horse drawn carriages that brought milk and chunks of ice twice a week to put in the ice box to keep our food cool. A big burly man would put a hooked clamp into the ice, hoist it on his ample, leather-covered shoulder, bring it into our house, and deposit it in the metal container. To this day, I still have to condition myself to say "refrigerator" rather than "icebox." There was one airstrip, Fleck's Field, outside of town, and on weekends we would go out there and stand outside the fence and wait for an occasional plane to take off or land. I had this deeply stirring desire to go where the planes went. Today, in the middle of the pandemic, with well over a million and a half air miles, I am grateful to stay home for Zoom programs. But then, it was like the cavalry riding by...a call, a summons, and I still love to fly though I hate airports.

The other small adumbration was the first television I ever saw. At night we might drive downtown to Herndon's Department Store, where the Lincoln-Herndon law office used to be, and in their side window was a box with a circular screen, probably 12 inches in diameter. On that tiny screen, miraculously, were talking heads from New York City. If a plane flew nearby the whole screen convulsed into jagged lines until the plane disappeared. We couldn't hear a word they said through the glass, but we stood there agape, stunned at the idea of live pictures coming through the air. Once again, I felt I needed to step into that larger world. My parents, lovingly, wished me to stay there forever, but I knew I had to leave, and I did.

Later, in a Wabash, Indiana hospital, as a college sophomore who was living for sports and not studies, I woke to a surgeon telling me my problem was something more than a torn cartilage from a cross block from a pulling guard in a game. "You have a degenerative bone disease, and not only are sports over, you won't be walking by the time you are forty." Well, at this hour, I am eighty-one plus, thanks to two knee replacements, and one hip, I walk every day for exercise, but I have lived in chronic pain all that time from that bone disorder. The cause is unknown. When I was born, I had a large thyroid, which literally threatened to choke me to death, so I was provided the most humane treatment of the time—massive radiation of the infant that shrank the thyroid. Many children who had that well-intended treatment have since died from a cancer in that locus. There are some who speculate that radiation affected my bones that way, but there is no real evidence to support that theory. So, lying there in the dark, wondering what I was to do with my life, I thought, with all the stunning wisdom of a sophomore (*Sophia*=wisdom + *moron*=moron), "I am in college. I guess I could become a student." And that turned a life around right there. More about that later.

Here is one other incident of which I am profoundly ashamed, of the many on my personal list. My father spent his life, not as a physician as he wished, but working on the assembly line of Allis-Chalmers. It was hot, oppressive, with the summer heat always in the triple digits as machinery generated enormous heat and the factory was several square blocks and too big to air condition. He and his comrades on the line were later rewarded for a lifetime of sacrifice working in a place with flying metal splinters, where one had to wear safety glasses all day, and steel-toed shoes, by having their pensions denied or cut to the bone when the Italian automaker Fiat bought A-C, cut costs, and finally closed the factory altogether, beginning Springfield's decline I suspect. (American companies apparently have to honor pension plans when buying a company, but foreign companies do not. I always wondered what geniuses in Congress figured that one out.) Anyhow, one hot August day when, lunch pail in hand, covered in industrial grease, and dripping from the intense heat, my father and I walked out together and I thoughtlessly said, "I am so glad September is here and I can go back to school." (That was still in my sports days, and my community had become my huddle mates and classmates.) My Father said, "For me, September never comes." He said it quietly, and utterly without rancor. One of his heroic acts was never to complain about his fate, and never to complain at all. (He did have migraine headaches that knocked him to his knees.) I felt awful and hated myself for such a thoughtless remark. I could get out, in large measure because of his work, and he never could. Not since being pulled out of eighth grade and being sent to work did he have a chance to pursue a dream. I dreamed *and* had the opportunity to leave town, see the world, and find my way in it. When he was on his deathbed later, I thanked him and told him much of what I did I did for him. I am not sure at that late hour he was fully able to understand what I said, but I surely hope so.

* * *

Now the point of these stories, and many more I do not plan to tell, is not self-indulgence here. I consider my life privileged to that lived by most folks in history, and certainly most folks on our planet at this hour. Each of the small moments made a large imprint upon me and have some wider applicability to us all. No doubt, our readers have similar examples, and I encourage you to bring them up into present awareness, record them, tell your children about them, and continue to process and brood what they might mean to you. I would like to try to illustrate a bit of that process to you now.

Going back to the beginning of this essay, the first point is to establish what intuitively we all know, namely, we all inherited not only a specific DNA, and a family of origin mélange of examples and influences, but the climate of the times as well. Some call it "cultural complexes," which are as real as any other we acquire in our journeys. It is as if all that we experience is going to pass through that atmospheric filter as well, and shape our sense of reality. The reader may wish to examine, perhaps do some research with relatives, siblings, newspapers, the internet files so available today, and establish what happened. How did you experience it at the time? How did that affect you? Any idea of what that experience made you do, or kept you from doing? How do you see it today; how do you reframe it from the adult's perspective? Is there unfinished business there? Is it possible that you might identify some stuck place, some deep current that runs with you still, perhaps still makes choices for you? Now, with the adult's much larger perspective, how can that be absorbed into your enlarged capacities to cope with life's tidal surges.

In talking about my experience of WWII, I note that I was safe, but the world around me was not, and that reality permeated my being and gave me a deep seriousness, a vague apprehensive view of the world, and burning desire to find out what really happened "out there." That persisting internal fire led me to visit Europe's major battlefields and six concentration camps: Dachau, Mauthausen, Bergen-Belsen, Buchenwald, and lastly, Auschwitz and Birkenau. My wife has asked not to visit any more of them, and I promised. But if we ever get back to Prague, I plan to go on my own to Theresienstadt. The first four were with my children as well, and the message of that horrid place—this is the *Endstation* of bigotry—was not lost on them at all. At Buchenwald, my wife and I walked through the *Straffenblock*, the punishment unit with its torture instruments. Just yards away, barely outside the barbed wire fence, was the playground for the children of the *SS* guards. At Auschwitz, the hanging scaffold was at the edge of the Commandant's home so his children might witness what went on there. Why did I drag these good souls there, to those places? I felt they needed to know, at least to know. And from childhood onward, I had to know the worst, to bear witness, and to feel an accountability wherever such suffering happens in our present world, as it keeps doing. This is why the child sang those songs on a street corner in a "safe city" so many years ago, and why it echoes in him still. What songs, sung or circulating below, sing in you, the reader?

I call it a "safe city," and yet a mad riot of white racist murders in Springfield, Lincoln's home town, in 1908, not unlike the mad slaughter of black Americans in Tulsa in 1921, one century after this writing, led to the formation of the National Association of Colored People, the NAACP. Perhaps, amid all these different, and separate evils, you too have something to grieve, something to address, something to respond to in this worrisome world. (During all my time in the *Land of Lincoln*, as our license plates proclaimed, I never heard one word, not one word, about the riots blocks from where I grew up.) What did your ancestors do, or fail to do?

What did mine? Don't ask if you are not willing to deal with something troubling. But only this telling of the truth gives us any hope for a cleansing future.

Secondly, we all had models. Some of them were very pathogenic and have hurt and haunted us our whole lives. We have to remember what happened then, literally, had nothing to do with us. But try to tell the child that. What happened, happened, and while it might have frightened us, directed or restricted us, it was not about us, really. So, it behooves us to ask, what were my models? What are they now? How do they support and empower me, or how do they denigrate and undermine me still? If I imagined Lincoln and Lou Gehrig as my idealized models, my daily examples were sometimes quite something else.

If there was any consistent message to me during those days, I now understand it as: life is difficult; it requires hard work always; don't expect anything you haven't personally earned; and you must try to be decent through it all. That is not a bad message, and it mostly describes my life. From my patients, I have seen quite other, more debilitating messages they had to live with. Our therapeutic work has focused on bringing up those latent messages from the distractions of daily life and to confront their explicit patterns to discern the tacit admonition or instruction to which they are service.

Thirdly, we all carry within us private stories, often secret stories of failure, moments of indecision and cowardice, times when we did something, or failed to do something, and it haunts us still. Welcome to the human species. As Mark Twain put it, we are the only animal that blushes, and has ample reason to. He also noted that we are the only animal that can be intentionally cruel. And he's a humorist. One wonders what a really crabby cynic might say.

Since these moments of shame, failure, regret haunt us anyhow, perhaps it behooves us to remember that in that hour, in that particular context, in that set of pressures, at that stage of our psychic life, we did the thing most reflexively protective. That we later judge it is a sign of an impressive growth of consciousness and moral accountability. What is pathological is to let it define one still. We are not what happened to us, and we are not what we did, then. We are rather what we facilitate, enact in the world today. I am of course not suggesting we turn a blind eye on those troubled hours, quite the contrary. But is it possible to turn a searing, white hot eye on one's dark moments and burn them out? Acknowledge them, remember to be accountable, remember to watch for their reappearance as bad actors in subsequent hours of decision and behavior. Remembering the past is the best way not to be bound to it. Being accountable to one's future, which is just as real, and heading toward us like the sun at dawn, is where the energy, focus, and locus of spiritual gravity has to shift.

Fourthly, life places various obstacles in our pathway. We probably all remember a child from our school days who died, or who had a debilitating disease. For them there was no life, seemingly. For the rest of us, hard times were coming, sooner or later. And the obstacles that life puts in our way also summon the heroic impulse that characterizes our species. Why did we climb those mountains, cross that heaving sea, stretch outward into space? Because that, too, is who we are. We want to know, we want to discover, learn, grow, engage. I do believe that one measure of our lives is what we made of them in the face of the obstacles fate placed in our way. To what degree was fate the dictator; to what degree did we open to, embrace, submit to our unfolding destinies; to what degree did we, in the convergence of those two force fields of energy step into life and fight?

I now look back on that bone disorder as a blessing. I did not at the time. It felt like a crushing defeat. But I had no future in sports, and the life of the mind and the path of the inquiring spirit opened as the alternative, and I am the richer for it. I did not know that a debilitating mid-life depression would cause me to look within, recover a different pathway forward, and lead to a richer life than I could ever imagined. Putting it most simply, for all the screw ups along the way, life gives you a gift. What do you plan to do with it?

Lastly, we must also review the wreckage of our biographies, and find gratitude. I cannot overly express how grateful I am that I have had from childhood onward the blessing of people loving me, quite apart from my merits, or without my earning that love. (Not having to earn love is what they call *grace*, and I acknowledge that gracefulness.) As Octavio Paz put it so succinctly and so sharply, "We are the playthings of time and accident; sickness and old age disfigure the body and cause the soul to lose its way. But love is one of the answers that humankind has invented in order to look death in the face."[34] And I do know there are many on this planet who never receive that gift.

I am also grateful for being born into a time and place in history where a child from a poor background can find a way. Remember Thomas Hardy's novel, *Jude the Obscure*, for a recent reminder of the psychospiritual cost of living in a culture where doors are closed. (The reaction to his truth-telling portrait was so vociferous in England that he gave up writing novels and spent the rest of his life writing poetry.) Most loved ones of mine, better human beings than I by far, have been felled by Time's obdurate scythe. Many in our world today, perhaps most, will never find their way through the thicket of oppression that blocks the expression of their possibilities. Whatever we have within or around us,

---

[34] Paz, *The Double Flame*, p. 160.

that can assist us to step into our own avenues of possibility, is to be celebrated. And, and...it constitutes a continuing accountability for us to live that privilege, that gift.

It is my hope that these brief notes toward a memoir are not seen as self-indulgent but rather serve as an invitation to the reader to deepen the scrutiny of your past. Our past is never really past. It is a continuing player in our present. Ask always the question: *What now is that making me do, or keep me from doing*? Then we gain greater purchase on the radical immanence of this hour with all its beckoning possibilities.

Each of us, as Rilke described in the headnote to this chapter, are sent out beyond recall, in search of the limits of our longing. That is what gives us our life, with all its promises, perils, and permutations. And that longing never ends until we do. So, dear reader, may you keep on longing, and keep on keeping on...out there, beyond recall to the old safe harbor, out there on the tenebrous and tormenting seas where there is no turning back.

Afterword
On the Matter of Soul

"Even a soul submerged in sleep is hard at work and helps make something of the world."

Heraclitus

Recently, a very thoughtful analysand asked this question, "What makes you think there is a soul?" I had never been asked that question before, and yet it seemed an honest and an obvious question to address.

Usually, when depth psychologists use the word *soul*, they mean it in a non-dogmatic way, as a translation of the Greek word *psyche*. Etymologically, it comes from two metaphors. One is "to breathe," suggestive of the invisible force that enters the newborn and departs at its demise. The second is linked to the "butterfly," suggesting the mysterious transformations of life, moving through phases, and emerging as both beautiful and ever elusive.

So much depends on how we frame that question: *Is there a soul*? What images come to mind? We can't posit an entity without calling up an image of it. Said image, objectifies it, renders it a noun, so to speak. If I say *chair*, you get an image of some "thing." If I say *soul*, perhaps you also get an image of something, albeit fuzzier than what came to mind with *chair*. This is why folks get so caught up, and heated up, on whether there is a God. For many, the idea posits an image; for others, that image is but an artifact of their map-making, image-generating mind. Where, or what, is the object of their projection, one might ask, since they have chosen a noun as the vehicle? If however, one thinks of these terms as verbs, namely, "as if" metaphors for something else, then one is properly in the realm of transpersonal mystery.

To say the gods *god*, i.e. go about *godding*, terrible as that sentence is, is closer to the possible truth. So, for the Christian, to pick one example of so many available, to think of the dogma of the ascension of Christ as a noun is one thing. As an object, then, Jesus's body would still be well within the range of our satellite and inter-planetary tracking devices. For the believer to think of it as a metaphor for entering into a timeless memory-event is altogether something else.

So, if one thinks of the soul as a noun, like the vas deferens, or the Isles of Langerhans, or the spleen, then it would show up on our CAT-scans. If one thinks of it as a metaphor for energy, for process, for function, then one is not bewitched by the image, not caught in a literalization that stultifies the idea altogether.

Years ago I had an academic colleague who told all his students that any time spent in analytic psychology was a complete waste because all would be proved to be neurology in the end. Now there was a man who was certain. And his certainty existed within the frame of his questions. Of course, all our experiences are neurologically registered, and are more or less measurable. But that is the easy part. What do we make of grief, of joy, or sorrow, of longing? These states of being are profoundly real, are neurologically recorded, and are something more than just neurological firings. In the nineteenth century, physiologists and philosophers did know what to make of *mind*. The brain was an obvious, tangible organ, but a function of that organ that could not only think but reflect upon itself reflecting constituted something called "mind." They couldn't solve the problem they named "the ghost in the machine." Well, we are a machine all right, and we have many ghosts, many ephemera knocking about inside.

The soul, then, may be seen as our metaphor for, our arrow pointing toward, our intimation of an energy within each of us. It not only governs the complex operation of our physiology, but expresses its autonomous will through emotions, symptoms, dreams, and the like. Apparently, it is an "organ of meaning," for we can bear anything when we have meaning, and be most miserable when we do not.

My second argument for the existence of what we call *soul* is love—love in all its forms: fierce, abiding, generative, self-sacrificing love. It includes love of partner, love of children, but also love of justice, fairness, beauty, excellence, and the pursuit of the soul's intent.

My third argument for the existence of what we call *soul* is very simple: music. Of course, I could choose any of the arts, especially writing, or painting, but I think music directly speaks to us from the soul. But why does it exist? It does not build the bridge nor mend the bone, and does not keep us from dying. Perhaps, as Louis Armstrong once said of jazz, "If you have to have it explained to you, you will never know." And, as Nietzsche added, "Without music, life would be a mistake." It resonates in our thumping heart, and tapping toe, and it exists in the rhythms of nature, the general diastole and systole of life and death. Perhaps in music our soul aligns with the archetypal rhythms which thrum through the fibers of being itself, echoing timelessly down the fleeting generations of human presence.

Elsewhere, in response to the question "what one thing I would send off on a space capsule to some alien species lusting to know who and what we were," I said: "a CD of the blues." What better can describe the human animal than that our tiny branch of the great evolving tree made the blues? Life is miserable: your wife went off with someone else; your children hate you; the rent is due; you don't have two dimes to rub together; rain is seeping through the roof; and your dog is looking at you with a funny expression—and so...and so, you pull out the guitar and make music. What better could describe the presence of some invisible but palpably driving energy that links us to the transpersonal?

Almost three millennia ago, the pre-Socratic Heraclitus said that even in our sleep, the soul is hard at work and labors to make something of this world. How did he know that? How do we know that? We live that mystery, each day, and if we have forgotten to pay attention to that wonder, then shame on us.

So, I ask the reader to listen to their favorite music. Or perhaps listen to Amethyst Kian and Her Chest of Glass sing "Trouble so Hard" on YouTube.com, or "Will the Circle Be Unbroken" with the Nitty Gritty Dirt Band, Johnny Cash, *et al.*, or Beth Hart and Jeff Beck's tribute to Buddy Guy at the Kennedy Awards Benefit, or Beethoven's Fifth Symphony, or the last movement of his Ninth. My list is very, very long, but you have your favorites. Listen to your list, observe yourself, feel, and then tell me you have no soul.

When I asked this question about soul to my friends Constance and Robert, this is what they emailed back: "For us, the idea of soul is to say there is something within us that wants to connect to a feeling that is independent of time and place. When we feel love we are transported out of our everyday experience. The same with anything that lifts us—music, dance, climbing a mountain, running in the Olympics—anything can be a personal soul experience. To be elevated, we think, can either be trivial or profound, but seems to be a desire for everyone."

They are zeroed in here. We all do need to feel some link to a transcendent dimension, to be part of a larger story than our ego's private journey. (What does it mean to "get high," after all, except to transcend the horizontal plane of one's life?) Many moons ago, Neo-Platonist Plotinus spoke of "the flight of the alone to the Alone." No matter what venue in which that quest occurs, it goes on in each of us, consciously or not.

What is the soul? You and I don't know what it is, nor do we have to, but we do know when it is present. We also know when we are separated from it. While it is true that we may find it difficult to see ourselves wholly in the broken mirror, it is also true that we may know that we are, nonetheless, seen...wholly seen.

Bibliography

Buchman, Lorne M. *Make to Know: From Spaces of Uncertainty to Creative Discovery*. London: Thames & Hudson, Ltd., 2021.

Caratenuto, Aldo. *The Difficult Art: A Critical Discourse On Psychotherapy*. Asheville, NC: Chiron Publications, 2013.

Dunn, Stephen. *Everything Else in the World*. New York: Norton and Norton, 2006.

_____. *Not Dancing*. Pittsburgh, PA: Carnegie-Mellon University Press, 1984.

Hollis, James. *Creating a Life: Finding Your Individual Path*. Toronto: Inner City Books, 2001.

_____. *Living Between Worlds: Finding Personal Resilience in Changing Times*. Boulder, CO: Sounds True, 2020.

_____. *Swamplands of the Soul: New Life in Dismal Places*. Toronto: Inner City Books, 1996.

_____. *The Eden Project: In Search of the Magical Other*. Toronto: Inner City Books, 1998.

_____. *Tracking the Gods: The Place of Myth in Modern Life*. Toronto: Inner City Books, 1995.

_____. *Under Saturn's Shadow: The Wounding and Healing of Men*. Toronto: Inner City Books, 1994.

_____. *Why Good People Do Bad Things: Understanding Our Darker Selves*. New York: Gotham/Penguin, 2007.

Hurd, Barbara. *The Epilogues: Afterwards on the Planet.* Berkeley, CA: Standing Stone Books, 2021.

Jung, Carl. *The Collected Works of C. G. Jung.* Edited by Herbert Read, Michael Fordham, G. Adler, and Wm. McGuire. Princeton: Princeton University Press, 1953-79 [abbreviated *CW* in this book].

_____. *Memories, Dreams, Reflections.* Edited by Aniela Jaffe. New York: Pantheon Books, 1961.

Paz Octavio. *The Double Flame: Love and Eroticism.* New York: Harcourt, 1995.

CPSIA information can be obtained
at www.ICGtesting.com
Printed in the USA
LVHW091200190122
708203LV00065B/1089/J